THE whole coconut

COOKBOOK

THE whole coconut

COOKBOOK

Vibrant Dairy-Free, Gluten-Free
Recipes Featuring Nature's Most
Versatile Ingredient

Nathalie Fraise

PHOTOGRAPHY BY ERIN SCOTT

TEN SPEED PRESS
Berkeley

· · · · · ·

INTRODUCTION

My love affair with coconut began while I was growing up on the island of Madagascar, where it was a regular staple in our cooking. Trucks piled high with coconuts made their way to the capital city, Antananarivo, where we lived. And when we traveled to the coast on vacation, we bought fresh coconuts from local children who harvested them directly from their trees. We drank the water, scooped out the meat for dessert, and used the coconut shells as bowls for the simple meals of freshly caught fish and fruit that we cooked on a fire by the beach. Coconut was an important part of our simple and natural lives back then, and my childhood memories of the fruit are both nostalgic and comforting.

Fast forward thirty years, and I have traded the beautiful red-earth island of Madagascar for the equally gorgeous but very different golden-green hills of Northern California. I have also radically changed my approach to food. A few years ago, I was living with chronic migraines and anxiety, and I had trouble maintaining a healthy weight. I knew something needed to change, and I looked to food to help me on my journey toward healing. After eliminating gluten, most dairy, alcohol, soy, chocolate, caffeine, and a few other foods, my health issues completely cleared up. I knew then that I was on the right track, and I haven't looked back since.

I had to look for healthy replacements for the foods I eliminated, though, and as I explored new ingredients, coconut started making a stronger appearance in my cooking. With all its creamy goodness, it's a natural and nutritious ingredient in countless recipes. It's more than a dairy, oil, flour, and sugar replacement; it can improve many recipes. Coconut milk is creamier and more flavorful than cow's milk; coconut cream makes the most beautiful whipped cream you have ever seen; coconut flour and oil work superbly in baking; coconut water is a wonderful addition to smoothies and juices; coconut aminos are a low-allergy replacement for soy sauce in savory dishes; and coconut palm sugar and coconut nectar are natural, lower glycemic sweeteners. Best of all? Cleaning up my diet and using coconut in my cooking has helped me feel better and more energetic than I have in years.

One of the beautiful properties of coconut is that it lends itself equally well to sweet and savory dishes, which is very rare for any ingredient, let alone a fruit. And not only is it tasty, it is truly one of nature's wonder foods, despite being high in saturated fat. For years people avoided coconut, afraid it would cause heart disease, but we now know that the fear was misplaced. It appears that saturated fats from healthy sources (coconut, raw butter, and pasturized eggs, for example) are actually very good for us. Moreover, coconut fat is different from other saturated fats in that it is mostly made up of medium-chain fatty acids (MCFAs), the most well known of which is lauric acid. MCFAs are metabolized differently from other saturated fatty acids in our diets: they go straight to the liver and are turned into energy instead of being stored as fat, thereby boosting metabolism and reducing appetite. Easily digested, these fatty acids are believed to help lower inflammation and to support the immune system and the brain. Lauric acid is a powerful antiviral, antibacterial, and antifungal fat; its concentration in coconut is unparalleled. It's so important to the human body that one of the few places it's found in significant amounts is in breastmilk—apparently, nature's way of making sure that babies get plenty of it.

Coconuts have been a staple food in many of the world's tropical and traditional cultures for thousands of years. I say it's time for all of us to start enjoying the benefits of coconuts in our diet. They are a very versatile ingredient, providing sustenance in myriad forms: coconut meat, coconut flour, coconut milk, coconut cream, coconut water, coconut oil, coconut vinegar, coconut palm sugar, coconut nectar, and coconut aminos. All of these products can be found in the recipes in this book, and I encourage you to experiment with them and find your own favorite ways to use coconuts in your own kitchen.

In general, you will find that the recipes in this book emphasize whole foods, minimally processed ingredients, and natural sugars. All the recipes are dairy- and gluten-free. For the omnivore recipes included, I offer suggestions on how to adapt them to a vegetarian diet. I only use unrefined sea salt in my recipes, and urge you to do the same.

A GUIDE TO COCONUT INGREDIENTS

Fresh young coconuts are the most natural—and best—way to consume coconuts. They are increasingly found in grocery stores, but tend to be much cheaper in ethnic food stores. Young coconuts should be chosen with care. Note how the outer shell looks: does it have any mold on it (pink or black), or cracks in the shell? If so, it might have spoiled. Shake the coconut and listen: you should hear the coconut water swishing inside the shell.

Once you bring your coconut home and are ready to open it, the easiest method uses a hammer and clean screwdriver. Lay the coconut on a kitchen towel to prevent it from slipping. Locate the two or three soft "eyes" on the shell, and rest the pointed end of the screwdriver on one of them. Then, using the hammer, gently strike the screwdriver to pierce a hole in the eye. Repeat into one other eye, and the water will easily pour out into a jar. Once you pour all the water out, either use the hammer or the butt of a chef's knife to crack the shell open and expose the coconut flesh, or meat. Note that when you open the coconut, it should smell fresh and clean, not at all fermented. The water should be fairly clear, not too opaque. If you notice any signs of damage, discard the coconut and use a different one.

What follows is specific information on coconut parts and ingredients. For more buying information, see pages 114–115.

COCONUT AMINOS Coconut aminos is a naturally fermented seasoning sauce made from aged coconut sap and mixed with sea salt. Rich in more than seventeen amino acids, it also has a nearly neutral pH, making it a great alternative to more acidic and highly allergenic soy sauce, to which it is similar in appearance though

MAKING COCONUT MILK AT HOME

To make coconut milk at home from fresh coconut meat, combine 2½ cups of chopped fresh coconut meat, from 1 to 2 coconuts, 4 cups of coconut water or filtered water (or both), and a pinch of sea salt in a blender. Blend on high until smooth, about 2 minutes. Strain through a nut milk bag into a bowl or jug; you'll get about 5 cups of milk. Discard the solids and refrigerate the milk for up to 5 days.

To make coconut milk from dried unsweetened coconut, combine 2½ cups of shredded coconut, 4 cups of very hot (but not boiling) water, and a pinch of sea salt in a blender. Remove the feeder cap from the blender lid so steam can escape; start the blender on the lowest speed. Blend on high until smooth, at least 5 minutes. Allow to cool, then strain through a nut milk bag into a bowl or jug; you'll get about 3 cups of milk. Discard the solids and refrigerate the milk for up to 5 days.

slightly sweeter in taste. Use coconut aminos anywhere you would use soy sauce. It works beautifully in Asian-inspired dishes and soups, in meat marinades, mixed with olive oil and lemon for salad dressing, drizzled over roasted vegetables for an extra kick, or used as a dipping sauce for sushi. Coconut aminos can be found in most health food stores.

COCONUT BUTTER Coconut butter (also sometimes called *coconut manna*) is coconut meat processed into a thick butter, much like nut butter. It can be used in place of regular butter—spread it on toast, add it to smoothies or your morning coffee, or use it in sauces or baking recipes for an extra nutritional boost. It's relatively easy to find in most grocery stores, and certainly in health food stores. Choose the least processed organic raw coconut butter—or make your own (see page 19)! Store the coconut butter at room temperature to preserve its creamy consistency.

COCONUT CREAM Coconut milk simply isn't creamy enough for some recipes—such as homemade coconut whipped cream—and that's where coconut cream comes in. Coconut cream is the thick cream that rises to the top of canned coconut milk when it is refrigerated for a few hours. Coconut whipped cream is one of the rare times when it is better to use *canned* coconut milk rather than boxed or homemade, because the cream in the boxed coconut milk rarely rises to the top. (There are ways to help get better whipped cream results with homemade coconut milk—like adding coconut oil to it to up the fat content—but these are far from dependable, so I don't bother.)

To separate the cream from the coconut water, simply refrigerate a can of coconut milk overnight (I like the Native Forest brand) carefully open the can and scoop the cream out with a spoon, leaving behind the watery part (which you can save and add to smoothies or juices).

COCONUT FLOUR Coconut flour is finely ground, defatted dried coconut meat, which means that it is not only gluten-free, but also grain-free. It adds a wonderful coconut flavor to baking recipes, but is a very thirsty flour, so the ratio of wet to dry ingredients will usually need adjustment when you're substituting it for other flours. For much more on the benefits of coconut flour, ways to use it in baking, and plenty of recipes, I highly recommend Bruce Fife's book *Cooking with Coconut Flour*.

COCONUT MEAT Coconut meat is the opaque white flesh of fresh coconuts. Coarsely chopped, it makes a great addition to many salads. It can also be added to smoothies, puddings, or cakes; or it can become the basis for coconut milk (see page 6). Its mild, creamy texture lends itself very well to so many dishes!

Some of the recipes in this book call for unsweetened dried coconut, which is simply dried coconut meat. It can be purchased in most grocery stores, and is usually available either shredded (smaller pieces the size of grated cheddar) or in flakes (larger pieces, like shaved parmesan). Other recipes use fresh coconut meat, which can be removed from the shell of a mature coconut, or can increasingly be found packaged, usually in the frozen section of natural foods stores or Asian markets.

COCONUT MILK Coconut milk is a thick, white, opaque milk made from pressed coconut meat mixed with coconut water or plain water (or a combination). None of the recipes in this book call for "light" or "reduced-fat" coconut milk; I believe in using foods in their most whole and natural form, so I always use full-fat. You may use boxed or canned coconut milk, but choose carefully. The relevant recipes in this book were tested using either my favorite boxed coconut milk brand, Aroy-D, or homemade coconut milk. Aroy-D's coconut milk tastes like the real thing. It's creamy without being gummy, and it's completely free of additives. I order cases of it online so I never run out. When I travel and Aroy-D is not available, I sometimes rely on canned coconut milk from Native Forest, as it is organic and comes in BPA-free cans. I firmly believe that homemade coconut milk is healthier than canned, as it does not contain any additives—preservatives, emulsifiers, and thickening agents are added to most commercial coconut milks to increase shelf life, prevent separation, and improve texture. So I always recommend looking at labels and choosing products that contain nothing besides coconut milk, coconut meat, and water. Or better still, make your own using the recipe on page 6! You'll need a nut milk bag. They can be purchased in most well-stocked grocery stores, or online. You could substitute with four layers of cheesecloth, but I highly recommend a nut milk bag, as it is much simpler to use.

COCONUT NECTAR Coconut nectar is the raw liquid sap of the coconut blossom. Relatively unprocessed, it is dark brown and has a thick, syrupy consistency. It is a rich source of minerals and amino acids and has a balanced pH. Like coconut sugar, coconut nectar is low glycemic—and it also doesn't taste much like coconut, but more like a mild sugar syrup with some caramel undertones. Because of its mildness, it's great for recipes that call for a more neutral-tasting sweetener.

COCONUT OIL Coconut oil is mostly saturated fat, yet it does not contain any cholesterol. Rich in the medium-chain fatty acid lauric acid (which has antiviral, antibacterial, and antifungal properties), it is believed to help strengthen the immune system, and to protect the heart by reducing inflammation and promoting healthy levels of cholesterol. Coconut oil also has a thermogenic effect, raising body temperature and boosting energy and metabolic rate. This is why coconuts help with weight loss. I prefer brands that store the oil in glass, such as the Artisana Brand.

With its mild, nutty flavor, coconut oil beautifully replaces other fats in many recipes, and can replace butter on toast or creamer in coffee. Because it is high in heat-stable saturated fats, coconut oil can withstand moderately high temperatures without oxidizing, which makes it easier to cook with than many other unrefined oils. It has a smoke point of about 350°F, so do not cook it higher than medium heat. Semisolid at room temperature, it may need to be melted before use in baking.

Always use organic, cold-pressed, raw, virgin coconut oil, and store it at room temperature. In cold temperatures, coconut oil solidifies and looks opaque, but it starts melting at 76°F. So, if you live in a warmer climate, it may always look clear and liquid.

As great as it is to use in the kitchen, coconut oil also shines for personal care. Among other things, it makes an ideal makeup remover, skin moisturizer, toothpaste, and, when mixed with baking soda, a very effective deodorant!

COCONUT PALM SUGAR Also known as coconut sugar, coconut palm sugar is made from dehydrated coconut flower nectar, so it doesn't taste much like coconut—it's nutty and slightly reminiscent of molasses or caramel. Brown in color, it is low glycemic, high in magnesium, potassium, and zinc, and less refined than most other sweeteners. Because of its increase in popularity, it is now easily found in most grocery stores. Replace refined sugar with coconut palm sugar in any recipe using a 1:1 ratio.

COCONUT VINEGAR Coconut vinegar is made from either coconut water or naturally fermented coconut tree sap called *tuba*, and is a slightly opaque, yellowish liquid. Using raw, unfiltered, unpasteurized coconut vinegar in our cooking allows our bodies to benefit from the beneficial bacteria found in the vinegar's fermenting "mother." Coconut vinegar works well anywhere one would normally use vinegar, such as in salad dressings, drizzled on roasted vegetables, added to homemade condiments, or even mixed into icy sparkling water, for a refreshing and nourishing shrub drink (see page 96). Coconut vinegar can be found in most health food stores and many grocery stores.

COCONUT WATER Coconut water is the nearly clear liquid found inside coconuts. It has a sweet, nutty taste slightly reminiscent of fresh coconut meat. I love to add it to smoothies or juices or even use it in lieu of water when making oatmeal. It makes a great post-workout drink, as it contains minerals and electrolytes. If you add a couple of tablespoons of chia seeds to a glass of coconut water, you've got yourself a light breakfast. Coconut water is believed to help balance blood pressure, prevent both acid reflux and kidney stones, and boost the immune system with its antiviral and antibacterial properties. Whenever possible, use water taken straight from a fresh coconut, or buy raw, unpasteurized 100 percent coconut water with no additives.

COOKING WITH COCONUT

Not only is coconut delicious, but its health benefits are truly impressive. It nourishes the body in ways that are rare in today's world of industrialized foods.

Nutritional value alone would not have been enough to keep me coming back to coconut, however. I am captivated by its near-magical versatility—the way I can use coconut products for almost any part of a finished meal, from flour to oil, milk to cream, aminos to vinegar, to sugar. This versatility, together with its irreplaceable flavor, gives an unlimited palette for culinary creativity.

In this book you will find many of my favorite ways to use coconut in all its many-faceted, satisfying, nourishing glory. I also invite you to keep experimenting with me—to find ever new ways to enjoy the whole coconut. I am thrilled to have you here on this journey.

•••

COCONUT YOGURT WITH RASPBERRY
POMEGRANATE COULIS AND TOASTED SEEDS 15

GRAIN-FREE FRUITY GRANOLA 17

CINNAMON BREAD 18

COCONUT BUTTER 19

BLACK BEAN AND CHARD QUINOA WITH TOMATO SALSA 20

BANANA CAULIFLOWER FARINA 22

CHOCOLATE HAZELNUT BUTTER 23

GRAIN-FREE RASPBERRY ALMOND MUFFINS 25

CREAMED SPINACH WITH FRIED EGG 26

AMARANTH PORRIDGE WITH STEWED VANILLA BERRIES 27

GRAIN-FREE PANCAKES WITH
ORANGE-VANILLA WHIPPED CREAM 28

BROCCOLI RABE, BUTTERNUT SQUASH,
AND TEMPEH SAUTÉ 31

BREAKFAST DISHES

Breakfast is the breaking of the overnight fast, and as such, it should be thoughtfully considered and planned. When the body has been busy resting, digesting, and detoxing all night, it needs to be replenished with high-quality nutrients that give it the fuel it needs to start the day. Our fast-paced culture and busy lifestyles place heavy demands on our bodies. Nourishing ourselves properly in the morning allows us to meet those demands with clarity and energy.

Along with protein, one of the most important components of a healthy breakfast is a good source of fat—which is why coconut, rich in beneficial fats, is ideal for this meal. When combined with a source of protein, such as nuts or an egg, coconut prevents the spikes in blood sugar that can trigger an energy roller coaster and moodiness, which means a much more pleasant and productive day.

Whether it's a grain-free fruity granola served with coconut milk (page 17), a nice plate of creamed spinach topped with a fried egg (page 26), warm cinnamon bread slathered with homemade coconut butter (page 18), or a cauliflower-banana Cream of Wheat (page 22), coconut for breakfast gives us sustained energy throughout the morning. So remember to include coconut in your breakfast routine, and you'll feel healthy and satiated.

Coconut yogurt tastes divinely tangy and creamy, and it can be used anywhere one would use dairy yogurt. Always use full-fat coconut milk free of additives to make coconut yogurt, as additives might damage the culture. Aroy-D coconut milk is a good choice.

When making coconut yogurt, it is important to add a little sweetener, as coconut milk is not very sweet and the probiotic bacteria in the yogurt need sugar to ferment properly. Coconut milk needs some sort of thickener, such as pectin, guar gum, or even tapioca starch to become yogurt; I prefer to use agar agar powder or unflavored grassfed beef gelatin.

COCONUT YOGURT WITH RASPBERRY POMEGRANATE COULIS AND TOASTED SEEDS

To make the yogurt, add the coconut milk and coconut palm sugar to a medium saucepan. Bring to a low boil over medium heat, then turn off the heat. Whisking vigorously and continuously for a couple of minutes, add the agar agar little by little and allow to dissolve. Let it rest and allow to cool to 110°F. You want the milk to be warm but not hot when you add the culture.

When the milk reaches 110°F, add the yogurt culture and mix well. Transfer the milk to a yogurt maker if you have one and follow the instructions for culturing. Or pour the milk into a very clean mason jar, cover with a kitchen towel secured with a rubber band, and place in an oven with only the light on. The light in the oven is usually enough to keep it at the ideal culturing temperature of 90°F to 110°F.

Allow the yogurt to culture for about 8 hours, then taste it. If you prefer a stronger cultured flavor, leave it to ferment for a couple

• • •

YOGURT

3 cups coconut milk

1 tablespoon coconut palm sugar or coconut nectar

2½ teaspoons agar agar powder (see Cook's Note, page 107) or grassfed beef gelatin

1 packet vegan yogurt starter culture or 1 teaspoon probiotic powder (see Cook's Note, page 16)

2 large pomegranates, seeded (see Cook's Note, page 16)

2 cups raspberries

3 tablespoons coconut palm sugar or coconut nectar

½ cup assorted seeds (such as sunflower, pumpkin, hemp, sesame), lightly toasted (see Cook's Note, page 16)

SERVES 4 TO 6

CONTINUED

more hours. Once it reaches your desired flavor, refrigerate for at least 8 hours. This will stop the fermentation process and allow the yogurt to thicken.

When you're ready to serve, make a coulis. Reserve about 1 cup of the pomegranate seeds for garnish and put the rest of the pomegranate seeds in a fine-mesh sieve over a large bowl. Press on the seeds with the back of a spoon to release the juice—it should yield about 1/2 cup juice. Discard the juiced seeds and put the juice, raspberries, and palm sugar in a high speed blender. Blend on high for a few seconds until smooth.

Serve the yogurt in bowls or glasses topped with the coulis, toasted seeds, and reserved pomegranate seeds. The coulis will keep for 3 to 4 days, refrigerated.

COOK'S NOTE To seed a pomegranate, slice it in half, hold each half cut-side down over a large bowl and, minding your fingers, hit the skin with a heavy spoon or meat tenderizer, releasing the seeds.

To toast nuts, seeds, or spices, preheat a sauté pan or skillet over medium heat. Add the nuts, seeds, or spices and toast, stirring often, until fragrant, 2 to 5 minutes depending on the size of the pieces. Pay attention, and once the nuts, seeds, or spices smell toasty and aromatic, whisk them off the heat and transfer to a cutting board or plate to cool completely—do not allow them to burn.

To ferment the yogurt, use either a yogurt starter culture (Cultures for Health offers a vegan culture) or some probiotic powder (available in health food stores). Do not add the cultures if the milk is very hot (use a thermometer to make sure it has reached the right temperature), or they will not survive and the yogurt will not ferment properly.

Granola is typically made with rolled oats mixed with different fruits and nuts, but oats can be difficult to digest, so I created this grain-free granola recipe that's easier on the digestive tract, but still delivers flavor and satisfaction. Feel free to experiment with different combinations of fruits and nuts, or double the recipe. If you would prefer to keep this granola completely raw, don't toast the coconut flakes.

GRAIN-FREE FRUITY GRANOLA

• • •

1½ cups dried unsweetened coconut flakes

2 cups mixed raw nuts (almonds, pecans, macadamias, hazelnuts), coarsely chopped

½ cup raw pumpkin seeds

½ cup golden raisins

¼ cup unsulfured dried apricots, coarsely chopped

¼ cup hemp seeds

¼ cup goji berries (see Cook's Note)

¼ cup cacao nibs (optional)

2 tablespoons coconut oil

1 teaspoon coconut nectar

1 teaspoon ground cinnamon

1 teaspoon vanilla extract

¼ teaspoon sea salt

Coconut milk or nut milk, for serving

Fresh fruit, for serving

MAKES ABOUT 6 CUPS

Preheat the oven to 350°F. Line a baking sheet with unbleached parchment paper. Spread the coconut flakes out on the sheet and bake until golden brown, 5 to 7 minutes. Coconut flakes burn easily. When they start to become golden on the edges, there is very little time left before they burn, so keep a close eye on them from that point on and pull them from the oven before they turn black and set them aside to cool.

In a large bowl, mix the coconut flakes, nuts, pumpkin seeds, raisins, apricots, hemp seeds, goji berries, and cacao nibs. In a small saucepan over very low heat, melt the coconut oil. Whisk in the coconut nectar, cinnamon, vanilla extract, and salt. Add the coconut oil mixture to the dried ingredients. Mix well with a wooden spoon.

Store in an airtight container in the refrigerator (it will keep for at least a couple of weeks) or freeze (for a couple of months) and bring to room temperature before using. Serve with coconut milk and fresh fruit.

➤ **COOK'S NOTE** Goji berries (or wolfberries) are small, red berries and one of nature's most nutritionally dense foods. Loaded with antioxidants, they are believed to increase longevity, vitality, and energy and help prevent cancer. Usually sold in dried form, they can be purchased in most well-stocked grocery stores or health food stores.

This bread has great texture and plenty of cinnamon flavor—
it does not last long in my house! Fortunately, it's easy to
make—no kneading and no rising—and it can be refrigerated
for a couple of days, then sliced and toasted for breakfast,
or a snack, anytime.

CINNAMON BREAD

・・・

Coconut oil

1¼ cups almond flour

¾ cup brown rice flour

3 tablespoons coconut
flour

¼ cup arrowroot starch

2 tablespoons psyllium
husk (see Cook's Note,
page 53)

2 teaspoons ground
cinnamon

1 teaspoon baking powder

1 teaspoon baking soda

½ teaspoon sea salt

½ cup coconut butter,
melted

⅓ cup coconut nectar

½ cup coconut milk

3 eggs, lightly beaten

MAKES ONE 8½ BY
4½ -INCH LOAF

Preheat the oven to 350°F. Line the bottom of an 8½ by 4½-inch
bread pan with unbleached parchment paper. Grease the sides with
coconut oil.

In a large bowl, whisk together the almond flour, brown rice flour,
coconut flour, arrowroot, psyllium husk, cinnamon, baking powder,
baking soda, and salt.

In a medium bowl, whisk together the coconut butter, coconut
nectar, coconut milk, and eggs until smooth.

Add the wet ingredients to the dry ingredients and mix well. Pour
the batter into the prepared pan and bake until golden brown and
a toothpick inserted in the middle comes out clean, 40 to 45 minutes.

Allow to cool in the pan for about 5 minutes before sliding a knife
along the sides to loosen the bread. Invert the loaf pan over a wire
rack to release the bread. Remove the parchment paper. Allow to
cool for another 10 minutes before slicing and serving. This bread
will keep, refrigerated, for about 5 days. After it's a day or so old,
slice and toast before serving.

Coconut butter is very easy to make at home. It is best made in a powerful blender, but if your blender is not very strong, or if you would like to speed up the process, simply add a couple of tablespoons of melted coconut oil to the shredded coconut. For flavor variety, add some vanilla, cinnamon, or even cacao powder to the butter.

. . .

5 cups unsweetened shredded coconut

Pinch of sea salt

MAKES ABOUT 1½ CUPS

COCONUT BUTTER

Combine the coconut and salt in a high-speed blender. Blend on low, slowly increasing the speed to high and scraping the sides as you go, until completely smooth, 3 to 4 minutes.

Store the butter in a glass jar at room temperature for up to 2 weeks. Storing it in the refrigerator will give it a longer shelf life, about 2 months, but let it come to room temperature before using.

COOK'S NOTE Coconut butter can also be made in a food processor, but it takes much longer—about 10 to 15 minutes—and the sides need to be scraped several times with a spatula.

• • •

SALSA

3 red or yellow heirloom tomatoes (about 2 pounds), coarsely chopped

½ large red onion, diced small

2 cloves garlic, minced

⅓ cup parsley, finely chopped

1 tablespoon olive oil

1 teaspoon lemon juice

Sea salt

Black pepper

1 tablespoon coconut oil

1 yellow or red onion, finely diced

Sea salt

¾ cup coconut milk

½ cup vegetable broth

2 cups quinoa, soaked overnight and drained

1½ cups cooked black beans

1 small bunch chard (about 8 ounces), center stalks removed, shredded

1 tablespoon lemon juice

Black pepper

Parsley, for garnish

SERVES 4 TO 6

Breakfast does not need to be sweet to be enjoyable. Eating a savory, high protein breakfast keeps our blood sugar levels balanced and gives us sustained energy (and stable moods) until lunch. If you are especially hungry, add a fried egg on top.

BLACK BEAN AND CHARD QUINOA WITH TOMATO SALSA

To make the salsa, combine the tomatoes, onion, garlic, parsley, olive oil, and lemon juice in a small bowl and season with salt and black pepper to taste. Set aside.

Preheat a large saucepan or Dutch oven over medium heat. Melt the coconut oil, then add the onion and a pinch of salt. Sauté, stirring occasionally, until the onion is translucent, about 5 minutes. Add the coconut milk and broth and bring to a boil. Stir in the quinoa, then return to a boil. Cover, and reduce the heat to low. Simmer until the liquid has been absorbed and the quinoa is cooked, about 15 minutes.

Stir in the black beans and chard and allow the beans to warm and the chard to wilt, about 2 minutes. Mix in half of the tomato salsa and the lemon juice. Season with salt and black pepper to taste. Serve immediately topped with the remaining salsa and garnished with parsley.

• • •

1 cup pecan halves

1 large head cauliflower, cut into florets

2 tablespoons coconut oil

2 tablespoons water

½ teaspoon sea salt

2 cups coconut milk

¼ cup coconut sugar

2 tablespoons maple syrup

1½ teaspoons ground cinnamon

1½ cups sliced bananas

2 tablespoons shredded coconut, for garnish

SERVES 4

Made from riced cauliflower, this grain-free porridge reminds me of farina (aka Cream of Wheat). It's packed with antioxidants and vitamins, and it's the perfect start to a busy day. Flavored with coconut milk, coconut sugar, maple syrup, and plenty of cinnamon, and topped with toasted pecans and bananas, it's a tasty and nourishing breakfast that will make you forget about grains. Prepare the riced cauliflower the night before to get a jumpstart in the morning.

BANANA CAULIFLOWER FARINA

Put the pecans in a medium skillet and toast until fragrant and starting to brown (see Cook's Note, page 16). Allow to cool, then chop coarsely. Set aside.

Put half the cauliflower florets in the food processor and pulse about 15 times, until it has the consistency of couscous or coarse cornmeal. Repeat with the other half of the cauliflower.

Place a large sauté pan over medium heat. Melt the coconut oil and add the cauliflower, water, and salt. Cook, stirring often, until the cauliflower is softer and almost caramelized, 6 to 8 minutes. Mix in the coconut milk, coconut sugar, maple syrup, and cinnamon until just warmed through.

Serve immediately topped with the bananas, toasted pecans, and shredded coconut.

• • •

2 cups hazelnuts

¼ cup coconut milk

¼ cup coconut oil

¼ cup coconut nectar

3 tablespoons raw
cacao powder

1 teaspoon vanilla extract

½ teaspoon ground
cinnamon

¼ teaspoon sea salt

MAKES ABOUT 1½ CUPS

There are days when breakfast means something rich, sweet, and reminiscent of childhood. When I feel this way, this chocolate hazelnut butter satisfies the craving while still providing many of the health benefits of coconut and only a small amount of sweetener. Spread it on toast or add a couple of tablespoons to a smoothie to boost both flavor and nutrition.

CHOCOLATE HAZELNUT BUTTER

Preheat the oven to 350°F. Line a baking sheet with unbleached parchment paper and spread the hazelnuts on it. Toast the hazelnuts until browned and fragrant, about 15 minutes—take care not to burn them. Allow them to cool slightly, then wrap them in a kitchen towel and rub them together to remove as much of the skins as possible (don't worry if some of the skins remain).

Transfer the hazelnuts to the bowl of a food processor and blend on high until very finely ground, about 2 minutes. Add the coconut milk, coconut oil, coconut nectar, cacao, vanilla, cinnamon, and salt. Continue blending until all of the ingredients are well incorporated and the butter is smooth, about 5 minutes.

Transfer to a mason jar and store at room temperature for up to 2 weeks.

These are a rare and beautiful thing: very satisfying grain-free muffins that taste perfectly balanced and achieve a bready texture without the use of any unhealthy gums. Once you try them, these babies will become a breakfast favorite in your house.

GRAIN-FREE RASPBERRY ALMOND MUFFINS

3 tablespoons chia seeds

¾ cup almond flour

¼ cup coconut flour

¼ cup arrowroot starch

¾ teaspoon baking powder

¾ teaspoon baking soda

¾ teaspoon sea salt

¾ teaspoon ground cinnamon

3 large eggs, lightly beaten

¼ cup coconut oil, melted

⅓ cup coconut nectar

½ cup coconut milk

1 tablespoon vanilla extract

½ cup unsweetened apple sauce

¾ cup raspberries, coarsely chopped

Nut butter or Coconut Butter (page 19), for serving

Honey or jam, for serving

MAKES 12 MUFFINS

Preheat the oven to 350°F. Line a muffin tin with unbleached paper cups.

Grind the chia seeds in a dedicated nut-and-seed coffee grinder. In a large mixing bowl, whisk together the chia seeds, almond flour, coconut flour, arrowroot, baking powder, baking soda, salt, and cinnamon; set aside.

In a medium bowl, whisk together the eggs, coconut oil, coconut nectar, coconut milk, vanilla, and apple sauce. Add the wet ingredients to the dry ingredients and mix well. Gently fold in the raspberries.

Pour about ¼ cup of the batter into each muffin cup. Bake in the oven until well browned on top, and a toothpick inserted in the middle comes out clean, 50 to 55 minutes. Allow the muffins to cool for about 5 minutes.

Serve warm with the nut butter and honey. Top with more raspberries, if desired. Store in an airtight container in the refrigerator for 3 to 4 days. Reheat in a 350°F oven for about 10 minutes.

Greens for breakfast—now that's a healthy way to start the day. And with the slightly bitter tang of creamed spinach mixed with runny yolk, these taste indulgent and heavenly. The recipe calls for what seems like a large amount of spinach, but it will greatly reduce when cooked.

CREAMED SPINACH WITH FRIED EGG

To make the sauce, whisk together the coconut milk, coconut butter, nutmeg, and salt in a small saucepan. Season with black pepper to taste. Bring to a boil over medium heat, then reduce the heat and simmer, stirring often, until the sauce has thickened up, and reduced by about half, about 15 minutes. Remove from the heat.

Preheat a large pot or wok over medium heat. Melt about 1 teaspoon of coconut oil and add the onion and garlic with a pinch of salt. Cook, stirring occasionally, until the onion is translucent, about 5 minutes. Add the sauce and the spinach in batches, tossing with tongs, until all of the spinach is wilted and most of the liquid has evaporated, about 10 minutes.

While the spinach is cooking, preheat a large sauté pan over medium heat. Melt 2 tablespoons of coconut oil. Crack the eggs into the pan, add salt and pepper to taste, and cook until the yolk is soft but the white is opaque, about 2 minutes.

Divide the creamed spinach between four bowls, top each with a fried egg, and serve immediately.

• • •

CREAM SAUCE

1½ cups coconut milk

2 tablespoons coconut butter

½ teaspoon freshly grated nutmeg

¾ teaspoon sea salt

Black pepper

Coconut oil

½ yellow onion, diced

1 clove garlic, minced

Sea salt

2 pounds baby spinach

4 eggs

SERVES 4

Amaranth is a very small seed that is high in protein, amino acids, calcium, and iron. It also contains a lot of fiber, but it is very easy to digest. It resembles the Cream of Wheat that some of us grew up with, but healthier, as it is a great source of fiber, minerals, and protein, as well as being gluten-free. Amaranth makes a hearty breakfast porridge whose nuttiness is beautifully complemented by gently stewed berries and crunchy nuts. Serve it with coconut milk or any other nondairy milk, such as almond or hazelnut.

AMARANTH PORRIDGE WITH STEWED VANILLA BERRIES

To make the berries, combine the berries, vanilla, and ginger in a medium saucepan over medium-low heat until the berries are gently bubbling and have rendered some of their juice, about 5 minutes. Turn off the heat so that you do not overcook. Taste, and add coconut palm sugar if needed.

Add the amaranth, coconut milk, coconut water, vanilla, coconut nectar, and salt to a medium saucepan. Bring to a boil, whisk in the cinnamon, cover, and simmer, stirring occasionally, until the milk is absorbed and the amaranth is soft, 30 to 40 minutes.

Serve the porridge immediately with more milk, if desired, topped with the berries and nuts. Store any leftovers in an airtight container and reheat with a bit more coconut milk or coconut water.

• • •

BERRIES

1 pound assorted berries, coarsely chopped

Seeds from 2 vanilla beans or 1 tablespoon vanilla extract

½-inch piece fresh ginger, peeled and minced

Coconut palm sugar

2 cups amaranth, soaked overnight, drained, and rinsed

3 cups coconut milk, plus more for serving

2 cups coconut water

Seeds from 2 vanilla beans, or 1 tablespoon vanilla extract

¼ cup coconut nectar

¼ teaspoon sea salt

2½ teaspoons ground cinnamon

1 cup pecans, almonds, or hazelnuts, or a mixture, toasted (see Cook's Note, page 16), coarsely chopped

SERVES 4 TO 6

This is really two recipes in one, but the coconut whipped cream complements the pancakes so well that it would have been a shame to separate them.

Coconut whipped cream makes a wonderful dairy-free topping for fruits, pies, and desserts of all kinds. This is one instance where I use canned coconut milk, as I have not had much luck making whipped cream from homemade coconut milk or from the Aroy-D brand, which comes in a box. However, I have had regular success with Native Forest canned coconut milk, so that is what I tend to use for this recipe.

GRAIN-FREE PANCAKES WITH ORANGE-VANILLA WHIPPED CREAM

• • •

ORANGE-VANILLA WHIPPED CREAM

1 can full-fat coconut milk

1 teaspoon orange zest

1 tablespoon coconut palm sugar

Seeds from 2 vanilla beans or 1 tablespoon vanilla extract

Pinch of sea salt

PANCAKES

2 tablespoons chia seeds

1/3 cup coconut flour

1/3 cup almond flour

1/4 cup arrowroot starch

1 teaspoon ground cinnamon

1/4 teaspoon sea salt

1/2 teaspoon baking soda

5 large eggs, whisked

2 tablespoons coconut nectar

1 1/2 cups coconut milk

2 teaspoons vanilla extract

Coconut oil

Fresh fruit, for serving

MAKES ABOUT TWELVE 4-INCH PANCAKES AND ABOUT 1 1/2 CUPS WHIPPED CREAM

To make the whipped cream, refrigerate the coconut milk along with a metal mixing bowl and the beaters from a hand mixer (or the whisk attachment for a stand mixer) overnight—you want everything very cold.

Open the can of coconut milk very carefully, making sure not to shake it. You do not want the cream to mix back together with the coconut water. Scoop out the top, creamy layer of coconut milk, which should be separated from the watery part, and transfer it to the chilled bowl. It should be very thick, almost solid. Save the coconut water to add to smoothies or juices.

Using a hand or stand mixer, beat the coconut cream until firm peaks form, about 3 minutes (don't worry, you can't overwhip coconut cream). Add the orange zest, sugar, vanilla, and salt to the cream, and beat again. Serve as a topping for fruit or pie, or anywhere you would normally use whipped cream. Store any leftovers in the fridge for about a week.

CONTINUED

To make the pancakes, grind the chia seeds in a coffee grinder dedicated to nuts and seeds. In a large mixing bowl, whisk together the ground chia seeds, coconut flour, almond flour, arrowroot, salt, and baking soda.

In a medium bowl, whisk together the eggs, coconut nectar, coconut milk, and vanilla. Add the wet ingredients to the dry ingredients and mix well. Allow the batter to rest for about 5 minutes.

Heat a griddle over medium-low heat. Melt a little coconut oil on it and pour ¼ cup batter per pancake, being careful not to overcrowd them. Cook on one side for 2 to 3 minutes, until the pancakes hold relatively firm when you try to lift them up with a spatula. Flip them over and cook until golden brown and well cooked inside, about 2 minutes more. Re-oil the griddle as necessary and keep the pancakes warm in the oven by covering them with a dish towel.

Serve immediately topped with fresh fruit and coconut whipped cream.

I find that grains often make me feel sluggish in the morning. This is why I tend to reach for savory, grain-free meals, as they keep me more energetic and alert. If you've never had broccoli rabe, be aware that it is bitter. Some people love it, others don't. If you don't care for its bitterness, feel free to replace with small broccoli florets instead.

BROCCOLI RABE, BUTTERNUT SQUASH, AND TEMPEH SAUTÉ

Heat a large Dutch oven over medium heat and melt the coconut oil in it. Add the onion and garlic with a pinch of salt. Cook, stirring, until the onion is translucent, about 5 minutes. Add the cumin, coriander, red pepper flakes, and turmeric and mix well. Add the butternut squash and cook, stirring often, until soft but still firm, about 5 minutes.

Add the coconut milk, vegetable broth, tomato paste, and broccoli rabe. Bring to a boil and cook until the broccoli is tender but still bright green, about 5 minutes. Mix in the tempeh and 2 teaspoons of salt; season with black pepper to taste. Serve immediately.

• • •

1 tablespoon coconut oil

1 yellow onion, diced small

4 cloves garlic, minced

Sea salt

1 teaspoon cumin seeds, toasted (see Cook's Note, page 16)

1 teaspoon coriander seeds, toasted (see Cook's Note, page 16)

¼ teaspoon red pepper flakes

½ teaspoon ground turmeric

4 cups butternut squash (about 1¼ pounds), diced

1 cup coconut milk

1 cup unsalted vegetable broth

1 tablespoon tomato paste

1 small bunch broccoli rabe (about 1 pound), chopped into bite-sized pieces

1 cup small-diced tempeh

Black pepper

SERVES 4 TO 6

. . .

MILLET, KALE, AND MISO-TEMPEH SAUTÉ 35

GRILLED SALMON ON CAULIFLOWER
AND BROCCOLI "RICE" 36

SPICY COCONUT CEVICHE 37

CREAMY VEGETARIAN POLENTA 38

VEGGIE COCONUT SUSHI HAND ROLL 40

BEEF, KALE, AND COCONUT RICE STUFFED PEPPERS 41

COCONUT, GINGER, AND CILANTRO MUSSELS 43

GREEN ONION PATTIES WITH SPICY PEANUT SAUCE 44

CREAMY RED LENTIL STEW 45

CHICKEN VEGETABLE THAI RED CURRY BOWL 46

PROVENÇAL AIOLI 49

OVEN-ROASTED CHICKEN THIGHS WITH
ZUCCHINI SPAGHETTI 50

COCONUT TORTILLAS WITH HERBED MUNG BEANS 52

LEMONY MUSHROOM RISOTTO 55

SWEET POTATO, SPINACH, AND CHICKPEA CURRY 56

MAIN COURSES

It is in main courses that coconut offers the most versatility, and perhaps the brightest place to shine. Coconut is a traditional ingredient in many beloved curries, soups, and stews as it complements a wide variety of textures and flavors and brings a characteristic richness. I play off of these familiar pairings in dishes like the Chicken Vegetable Thai Red Curry Bowl (page 46), Creamy Red Lentil Stew (page 45), and Millet, Kale, and Miso-Tempeh Sauté (page 35).

But coconut can also be a successful ingredient in unexpected places, adding flavor and depth to recipes such as Lemony Mushroom Risotto (page 55), Creamy Vegetarian Polenta (page 38), and Provençal Aioli (page 49). It consistently enhances dishes in surprising ways, allowing me to see some of my favorite recipes in a new light. For example, I didn't think I would enjoy the taste of coconut in mushroom risotto, thinking it would compete with the other flavors in an unpleasant way. I gave it a try anyway and was pleasantly surprised that coconut worked perfectly in the dish, combining with the flavors seamlessly. It made for one of the best tasting risottos I had ever had!

I say this so that you are encouraged to try coconut in places that you might not have considered before. Try coconut oil in your coffee, for example, or anywhere you might normally use butter (such as on toast or for popcorn), or add coconut milk to creamy sauces on pasta. I know you will be as surprised and delighted as I was at how well coconut complements such a wide variety of dishes.

This millet sauté holds the most nourishing combination of nuttiness and flavor. Millet is a gluten-free grain whose texture and taste is reminiscent of old world earthiness. Cooked here in coconut milk, and accented by mushrooms, kale, tempeh, and cherry tomatoes, this dish is colorful, and über healthy. To yield the best results, do not stir the millet while it is cooking. It is happiest, and cooks most evenly, when left alone. The miso should provide ample saltiness to this dish, but feel free to add some salt, if desired.

MILLET, KALE, AND MISO-TEMPEH SAUTÉ

• • •

1½ cups millet

2 tablespoons coconut aminos

¼ cup red miso

3 tablespoons lime juice

1½ cups coconut milk

1½ cups vegetable broth

2 tablespoons coconut butter

1 pound mixed mushrooms, coarsely chopped

1 bunch lacinato kale (about 8 ounces), center veins removed, shredded

2 cloves garlic, minced

3 green onions, finely sliced

2 teaspoons finely chopped jalapeño (optional)

1½ cups finely diced tempeh

2 cups cherry tomatoes, halved

½ cup cilantro, finely chopped

½ cup parsley, finely chopped

Black pepper

½ cup coconut flakes, toasted (see Cook's Note, page 16)

SERVES 4 TO 6

In a dry skillet over medium heat, toast the millet until fragrant, about 3 minutes. Set aside.

Whisk together the coconut aminos, miso, and lime juice. Set aside.

In a large pot or Dutch oven over medium heat, bring the coconut milk and broth to a boil. Add the millet and stir, then reduce the heat to very low, cover, and cook for about 25 minutes, stirring once midway through. Uncover, add the coconut butter and the coconut aminos mixture, and mix well. Add the mushrooms, kale, garlic, green onions, and jalapeño and cook, stirring often, until the mushrooms are soft, about 5 minutes.

Stir in the tempeh and heat until warm, about 2 minutes more. Add the tomatoes, cilantro, and parsley. Season with black pepper to taste.

Transfer to a serving platter and top with the coconut flakes. Serve immediately.

You might already be familiar with cauliflower "rice" (see page 22)—"rice" can be made out of broccoli, too. This mixture of both is wonderful: lemony, creamy, and perfect with grilled wild salmon.

GRILLED SALMON ON CAULIFLOWER AND BROCCOLI "RICE"

· · ·

1 head broccoli (about 1 pound), cut into small pieces

1 head cauliflower (about 1 pound), cut into small pieces

1 cup dried shredded coconut

3 green onions, white and green parts, finely chopped

2 cups coconut milk

3 tablespoons coconut butter

Zest of 2 limes

Juice of 2 limes

Sea salt

¼ cup dill, finely chopped, plus more for garnish

Black pepper

2 tablespoons coconut oil

4 wild salmon fillets, about 4 to 5 ounces each

SERVES 4

Fill the bowl of a food processor no more than halfway with broccoli and cauliflower florets—you will need to do this step in batches. Pulse until the broccoli and cauliflower have the consistency of couscous or quinoa (the broccoli will remain slightly more stringy than the cauliflower). Transfer to a Dutch oven or large sauté pan, and repeat until all the broccoli and cauliflower is chopped up and in the pan.

Add the shredded coconut, most of the green onions (save a little for garnish), coconut milk, coconut butter, lime zest and juice, and 1 teaspoon of salt to the Dutch oven. Cook on medium-high heat, stirring very often, until the vegetables have softened but the broccoli is still bright green, 6 to 8 minutes. Stir in the dill.

While the broccoli and cauliflower are cooking, prepare the salmon. Season the salmon fillets with salt and pepper on both sides. Heat a large skillet or sauté pan over medium-high heat and melt the coconut oil in it. Add the salmon fillets to the pan and cook until golden-brown on the outside but still rare on the inside, 2 to 3 minutes per side, depending on the thickness of the fillets.

Divide up the broccoli and cauliflower "rice" among four plates and place the salmon on top. Sprinkle with the reserved green onion and dill. Serve immediately.

• • •

1½ pounds sushi-grade ocean white fish (such as halibut, seabass, snapper, cod), cut into ½-inch cubes

½ red onion, finely diced

1 clove garlic, minced

Zest of 1 lime

1 cup lime juice

¼ cup coconut vinegar

1-inch piece fresh ginger, peeled and minced

½ jalapeño, top removed, minced (optional)

1½ teaspoons sea salt

1 large tomato, finely diced

1 small red bell pepper, stem, ribs, and seeds removed, finely diced

½ cucumber, seeded and finely diced

½ cup coconut milk

⅓ cup finely chopped cilantro, plus more for garnish

SERVES 4 TO 6

Ceviche is a classic South American raw fish dish that is perfect for hot summer days when turning on the stove does not sound very appealing. I like to mix more vegetables into the ceviche than is traditional. Since the fish will be consumed raw, make sure that it is incredibly fresh. It should not smell fishy or feel slimy, and if the head is still on, the gills should be bright red and the eyes clear.

SPICY COCONUT CEVICHE

In a large glass bowl, mix together the fish, onion, garlic, lime zest, lime juice, coconut vinegar, ginger, jalapeño, and salt. Allow to marinate, in the refrigerator, until the outer layers of the fish look opaque, about 50 to 60 minutes. Mix in the tomato, bell pepper, cucumber, coconut milk, and cilantro. Divide among 4 to 6 bowls and top with extra cilantro. Serve immediately.

Oh, my. This creamy polenta is so easy to make, and very, very addictive. It's pure comfort food. Topped with sautéed vegetables and lentils, it makes a substantial meal.

CREAMY VEGETARIAN POLENTA

• • •

3 cups coconut milk

2 cups vegetable broth, preferably homemade

Sea salt

1 cup polenta

2 tablespoons coconut butter

2 tablespoons nutritional yeast

Black pepper

2 tablespoons coconut oil

2 large leeks, white and light green parts, finely chopped

2 cloves garlic, minced

1 bunch asparagus, tough ends removed, chopped into 1-inch pieces

1 cup shelled green peas

2 cups chopped tomatoes

1 tablespoon lemon juice

1 cup cooked lentils

1/2 cup parsley, finely chopped, plus extra for garnish

2 tablespoons olive oil

SERVES 4 TO 6

In a large saucepan or Dutch oven, combine the coconut milk, broth, and 1½ teaspoons of salt. Bring to a boil over medium-high heat. Add the polenta, trickling it into the liquid like rain and whisking vigorously the whole time. Reduce the heat to bring to a low simmer, and cook, uncovered, whisking vigorously several times so the polenta doesn't clump, until the polenta is soft, 45 to 55 minutes. Add the coconut butter and nutritional yeast. Sprinkle the black pepper to taste. Mix well.

While the polenta is cooking, heat a large sauté pan or wok over medium heat. Melt the coconut oil, then add the leeks and garlic with a pinch of salt. Cook, stirring often, until the leeks are soft but not browned, about 5 minutes. Add the asparagus and cook, stirring often, until bright green and still firm, about 3 minutes. Add the peas, tomatoes, lemon juice, lentils, and about 1½ teaspoon of salt (or to taste) and cook long enough to warm everything through, about 2 minutes. Stir in the parsley.

When the polenta is done, top it with the vegetables and lentils. Sprinkle with the extra parsley and drizzle with the olive oil. Serve immediately.

These hand rolls are made with cauliflower chopped to the size of rice grains, so they are not only vegan but also completely grain-free. They make for a very light lunch or dinner, so if you would prefer something more substantial, add a heftier source of protein, such as raw fish or tempeh. There is no "right" filling for these—use anything that strikes your fancy. Making a hand roll can be a little tricky, but you will soon get the hang of it. Alternatively, use full nori sheets and make regular rolls (see page 110).

VEGGIE COCONUT SUSHI HAND ROLL

(see page 110)

To make the dipping sauce, mix together the coconut aminos and ginger. Set aside.

Put the cauliflower in the bowl of a food processor. Pulse 10 to 15 times, until it looks like rice. Transfer to a large sauté pan over medium heat. Add the vinegar, water, sugar, and a couple pinches of salt and mix well. Cook, stirring often, until the cauliflower is soft, about 5 minutes. Set aside to cool completely.

Lay half a sheet of nori on your left hand. Scoop about 2 tablespoons of cauliflower rice onto the nori in your left hand. Spread it out with wet fingers, but leave about a 1/2-inch margin of nori around the edges. Sprinkle the cauliflower with gomasio and place a small amount of coconut meat, cucumber, and avocado in the center of the cauliflower rice. Working on the diagonal, roll the bottom left hand corner of the nori sheet over the rice and filling. Tuck the bottom of the nori in while you roll. When you're done rolling, dab a little water on the edges of the nori to hold the roll together. Repeat with the other nori sheets and filling, and serve immediately with the sauce on the side.

• • •

DIPPING SAUCE

1/4 cup coconut aminos

3-inch piece ginger, minced

1 head cauliflower, cut into small florets

1/4 cup coconut vinegar

1/4 cup water

2 tablespoons coconut palm sugar

Sea salt

8 sheets nori, halved

Gomasio (a sesame seed condiment, optional)

1 cup fresh coconut meat, thinly sliced

1 cucumber, seeded and thinly sliced

1 avocado, thinly sliced

SERVES 4

• • •

RICE

1 cup brown basmati rice, soaked overnight, rinsed, and drained

1 cup coconut milk

¼ cup water

1 teaspoon lime zest

1 tablespoon lime juice

1 teaspoon sea salt

Black pepper

FILLING

1 tablespoon coconut oil

½ yellow onion, diced

Sea salt

5 cloves garlic, minced

1 pound ground beef

½ cup tomato purée

1 teaspoon freshly grated nutmeg

2 teaspoons paprika

¼ teaspoon cayenne pepper (optional)

2 cups kale (about 4 leaves), finely chopped

1 tablespoon lime juice

Black pepper

½ cup parsley, finely chopped

3 red bell peppers

3 yellow bell peppers

¼ cup pine nuts

SERVES 6

These colorful peppers are the perfect one-dish main course. Stuffed with creamy coconut rice, spicy sautéed ground beef, and health-supportive kale, they are festive and nourishing. Serve them with a simple green salad for a very complete meal.

BEEF, KALE, AND COCONUT RICE STUFFED PEPPERS

To make the rice, in a medium saucepan over medium-high heat, combine the coconut milk, water, lime zest, lime juice, and salt. Season with black pepper to taste. Bring to a boil. Stir in the rice, reduce the heat to low, cover, and simmer until the rice is cooked, about 10 minutes. Remove from the heat and set aside.

Meanwhile, make the filling. Preheat the oven to 375ºF. Heat a large sauté pan over medium-high heat and melt the coconut oil. Add the onion and a pinch of salt. Cook, stirring often, until the onion is translucent, about 5 minutes. Add the garlic and ground beef and cook, breaking up the meat with a fork, until the beef is no longer pink and most of the liquid has evaporated, about 10 minutes. Add the tomato purée, nutmeg, paprika, and cayenne. Cook for another 1 to 2 minutes to allow the flavors to combine.

Mix in the kale and lime juice and allow the kale to wilt, about 1 minute. Mix in the rice and turn the heat off. Season with salt and pepper to taste. Add the parsley and stir.

Slice the tops off of the peppers. Remove and discard the ribs and seeds. Place the peppers, cut-side up, in a shallow baking dish. Fill the peppers with the meat and rice mixture and sprinkle with the pine nuts. Place the tops between the peppers. Bake until the pine nuts are golden, 25 to 35 minutes.

Transfer the peppers to a serving dish and replace the tops; serve immediately.

Cooking mussels can feel intimidating, but I assure you that this dish is one of the easiest you will ever make. Once the mussels are cleaned, the whole thing comes together very fast, allowing you to impress your family and guests with minimal effort. The flavor is so addictive you will find yourself wanting to make it over and over again.

COCONUT, GINGER, AND CILANTRO MUSSELS

Scrub the mussels with a vegetable brush under cool running water. Pull off any stringy beards and discard any mussels that have a broken shell or that are open and will not close when tapped.

Place a large pot over medium heat and melt the coconut oil. Add the leeks, ginger, garlic, and a pinch of salt. Cook, stirring often, until the leeks are very soft, about 5 minutes. Stir in the coconut milk, broth, juice, and wine and bring to a boil. Add 1 tablespoon of salt and season with black pepper to taste.

Add the mussels to the pot and bring to a boil. Cover and cook over medium-high heat, stirring occasionally, until the mussels open, about 8 to 10 minutes (throw away any that don't open). Stir in the chopped cilantro and basil and transfer to a serving platter. Garnish with the extra basil and cilantro and serve immediately.

• • •

6 pounds mussels

2 tablespoons coconut oil

2 leeks, white and light green parts, finely chopped

2-inch piece of fresh ginger, peeled and minced

5 cloves garlic, minced

Sea salt

3 cups coconut milk

1 cup vegetable broth

2 tablespoons lemon juice

1 cup white wine

Black pepper

1 cup basil, finely chopped, plus more for garnish

1 cup cilantro, finely chopped, plus more for garnish

SERVES 4 TO 6

These crispy, flavor-filled onion patties pair perfectly with the spicy peanut sauce. The sauce! It will make you want to lick the bowl. Serve with a side salad for a light lunch or dinner.

GREEN ONION PATTIES WITH SPICY PEANUT SAUCE

. . .

SAUCE

¼ cup crunchy peanut butter

3 tablespoons sesame oil

1 tablespoon plus 1 teaspoon coconut aminos

1 tablespoon coconut vinegar

1 tablespoon lime juice

2 teaspoons coconut nectar

1 teaspoon cayenne pepper

½ teaspoon sea salt

GREEN ONION PATTIES

1 cup almond flour

2 tablespoons coconut flour

1 tablespoon psyllium husk (see Cook's Note, page 53)

3 eggs, whisked

4 green onions, white and green parts, finely chopped

1 small zucchini, grated

¼ teaspoon sea salt

Black pepper

1 tablespoon coconut oil

SERVES 4

To make the sauce, whisk together all of the ingredients in a bowl until well incorporated. Set aside.

To make the green onion patties, in a large bowl, whisk together the almond flour, coconut flour, and psyllium. In a medium bowl, whisk together the eggs, green onions, zucchini, and salt. Season with black pepper to taste. Add the egg mixture to the flour mixture and mix well. Using your hands, shape the mixture into four round, flat patties. Set aside on a plate.

Heat a griddle over medium heat and melt the coconut oil. Add the patties, in batches if necessary. Cook until each patty is cooked through and golden brown on both sides, about 2 minutes per side.

Serve immediately with the sauce on the side.

This is a weekday or weekend dish for those times when you don't want to spend a lot of time in the kitchen but still want something very nourishing to carry you through. Spiced lentils, cooked in chicken broth and coconut milk complemented by chopped kale, are the perfect topping for cauliflower "rice" (see page 22) or cooked quinoa.

CREAMY RED LENTIL STEW

Heat a Dutch oven or stockpot over medium heat and melt the coconut oil. Add the onion, garlic, and ginger with a pinch of salt. Cook, stirring often, until the onions are translucent, about 5 minutes.

Add the cumin, turmeric, and coriander and cook until fragrant, about a minute. Add the lentils, celery, carrots, jalapeño, and chicken broth and cook, covered, until the carrots are tender, 10 to 12 minutes. Add the coconut milk and lemon juice and stir well.

Stir in the kale and allow to soften, about 2 minutes. Season with salt and pepper to taste. Right before serving, mix in the cilantro.

...

1 tablespoon coconut oil

1 medium yellow onion, finely diced

3 cloves garlic, minced

1-ince piece fresh ginger, peeled and minced

Sea salt

1 teaspoon cumin seeds

1 teaspoon ground turmeric

1/2 teaspoon ground coriander

1 1/2 cups red lentils, rinsed

1 celery stalk, thinly sliced

3 medium carrots, scrubbed and thinly sliced

1/2 small jalapeño pepper, finely chopped (optional)

3 1/2 cups unsalted chicken or vegetable broth, preferably homemade

1 cup coconut milk

2 tablespoons lemon juice

2 cups finely chopped kale (from about 4 leaves)

Black pepper

1/3 cup chopped cilantro

SERVES 4 TO 6

• • •

1 tablespoon coconut oil

½ yellow onion, diced

Sea salt

2-inch piece fresh ginger, peeled and minced

2 cloves garlic, minced

3½ cups coconut milk

¼ cup red curry paste

¼ cup lime juice

½ lemongrass stalk, cut diagonally in 2 or 3 pieces and bruised with a mallet

2 kaffir lime leaves

2 tablespoons coconut aminos

1 tablespoon fish sauce

3 chicken breasts, cut into bite-sized pieces

½ head cauliflower, cut into small pieces

½ head broccoli, cut into small pieces

2 large carrots, scrubbed and sliced into bite-sized pieces

½ cup peas

¼ cup chopped cilantro, plus more for garnish

⅓ cup chopped basil, plus more for garnish

Cooked brown rice noodles or brown rice

SERVES 4 TO 6

When we think of coconut-based main dishes, we often think of curries, and for good reason. Creamy coconut milk blended with any type of curry blend yields a perfectly spiced and flavored sauce or soup that is difficult to resist. Kaffir lime leaves can be found in well stocked grocery stores or Asian grocers. To keep this dish vegetarian, replace the chicken with your vegetarian protein of choice, and replace the fish sauce with coconut aminos (though do be aware that fish sauce gives Thai dishes a unique taste that is difficult to replicate).

CHICKEN VEGETABLE THAI RED CURRY BOWL

Heat a large Dutch oven over medium-high heat. Melt the coconut oil, and add the onion and a pinch of salt. Cook, stirring often, until the onion is translucent, about 5 minutes. Add the ginger, garlic, coconut milk, curry paste, lime juice, lemongrass, and kaffir lime leaves. Bring to a boil, reduce the heat, cover, and simmer until thickened and reduced by one-third, 12 to 15 minutes. Whisk in the coconut aminos and fish sauce.

Add the chicken, cauliflower, broccoli, and carrots. Cook until the chicken is cooked through but not dry and the vegetables are just tender but still brightly colored, 5 to 7 minutes. Turn off the heat. Add the peas, cilantro, and basil. Using tongs, fish out the lemongrass and kaffir lime leaves and discard. Taste and add more coconut aminos or fish sauce if you'd like a saltier taste.

Serve immediately over the noodles with the extra cilantro and basil sprinkled on top.

Aioli is both a sauce and a dish from the South of France. The sauce is similar to mayonnaise, and is typically made with olive oil, garlic, lemon juice, egg yolk, and salt. The dish, also called "Le Grand Aioli," is a large platter of cold steamed vegetables, hard-boiled eggs, and sometimes smoked fish, served with aioli on the side. Using coconut meat in lieu of the usual egg yolk in the sauce gives the dish a unique creamy flavor, while still hewing to the color and texture of a more traditional aioli. The components of this dish can (and even should) be prepared ahead of time, as it is served cold.

PROVENÇAL AIOLI

To make the aioli, combine the coconut meat, coconut milk, garlic, mustard, lemon juice, salt, turmeric, and a grind or two of black pepper in a high-speed blender. Process on high until smooth, about 1 minute, and the consistency of mayonnaise. If the mixture is too dry and the blender stalls, add a little more coconut milk, a tablespoon at a time, until the mixture is wet enough to blend.

Cut and arrange the steamed and raw vegetables, potatoes, and eggs on a serving platter, with the aioli in a bowl on the side.

* * *

AIOLI

1 cup coarsely chopped coconut meat

½ cup coconut milk

4 cloves garlic

½ teaspoon Dijon mustard

1 teaspoon lemon juice

1½ teaspoons sea salt

Pinch of ground turmeric

Black pepper

Steamed vegetables (cauliflower, broccoli, carrots), cold

Raw vegetables (zucchini, cucumber, peppers)

Cooked new or fingerling potatoes, cold

Hard-boiled eggs, cold

SERVES 4 TO 6 (MAKES ABOUT 1 CUP AIOLI)

How do we get the taste of cheese without the dairy? In many cases, nutritional yeast does the trick. Nutritional yeast is flakes of deactivated yeast that impart a nice cheesy flavor to dishes. It can be found in most well-stocked grocery stores or health food stores. Feel free to use grated Parmesan, if you would prefer. To make the zucchini spaghetti, use a spiralizer, vegetable slicer, or mandoline; or you can also slice the zucchini with a sharp knife, which will turn it into linguine instead!

OVEN-ROASTED CHICKEN THIGHS WITH ZUCCHINI SPAGHETTI

• • •

6 chicken thighs

Coconut oil or ghee

Sea salt and black pepper

8 medium zucchini (about 3½ pounds total), ends trimmed

2 cups coconut milk

2 tablespoons coconut butter

2 green onions, white and green parts, finely chopped

3 cloves garlic, minced

¼ cup nutritional yeast

⅓ cup basil, finely chopped

¼ cup parsley, finely chopped

SERVES 6

Preheat the oven to 450°F. In a baking dish, lay the chicken thighs skin-side up in a single layer. Spread a generous amount of coconut oil over each thigh and season well with salt and pepper. Bake until the chicken skin has browned and crisped and the meat is cooked through but not dry, 40 to 45 minutes. Remove from the oven and allow to rest for about 5 minutes.

While the chicken is cooking, bring a large pot of salted water to a boil.

Make spaghetti-thin strands out of the zucchini using a spiralizer or mandoline. It will seem like a large amount, but it reduces when cooked. In a medium saucepan, combine the coconut milk, coconut butter, green onions, garlic, and nutritional yeast. Season with salt and black pepper to taste. Bring to a boil over medium-high heat, then lower the temperature and simmer gently until reduced by about half, about 15 minutes.

Add the zucchini to the boiling water, and cook until softened but still al dente, about 2 minutes. Drain and return to the pot. Drizzle the sauce onto the zucchini and toss, making sure the zucchini is well coated. Right before serving, mix in most of the basil and parsley, then transfer to a serving dish along with the chicken thighs and sprinkle the rest of the basil and parsley over the top.

If you are trying to eat less grains and have been missing certain foods, like tortillas, look no more! When topped with mung beans, cherry tomatoes, and lots of herbs, these wonderfully moist coconut tortillas make a very simple, but very healthy lunch. Prepare the tortillas and filling in advance, and simply reheat before serving for a quick meal on the go.

COCONUT TORTILLAS WITH HERBED MUNG BEANS

¾ cup mung beans, soaked overnight, rinsed, and drained

1½ cups finely chopped mixed herbs (such as basil, cilantro, parsley), plus more for garnish

¼ red onion, finely diced

4 cups cherry tomatoes, quartered

1 tablespoon olive oil

2 teaspoons sea salt

Black pepper

TORTILLAS

1½ cups coconut milk

3 eggs, whisked

¼ cup almond flour

3 tablespoons coconut flour

3 tablespoons whole psyllium husks (see Cook's Note)

½ teaspoon baking powder

½ teaspoon sea salt

Black pepper

Coconut oil

SERVES 6

Fill a medium saucepan with water and bring to a boil over high heat. Add the mung beans, reduce the heat to a simmer, and cook, uncovered, until tender, 20 to 25 minutes, skimming off any foam that may rise to the surface. Drain and add the herbs, onion, tomatoes, olive oil, and salt. Season with black pepper to taste. Set aside.

To make the tortillas, whisk together the coconut milk and eggs in a medium bowl. In a large bowl, whisk together the almond flour, coconut flour, psyllium, baking powder, salt, and a grind or two of black pepper. Add the wet ingredients to the dry ingredients, trickling the mixture in like rain and mixing continuously until well incorporated. Let the batter stand for 7 to 10 minutes, until thickened.

Heat a griddle or large skillet over medium heat and melt about 1 tablespoon of coconut oil in the pan. Pour about ⅓ cup of batter into the skillet and use the back of a spoon to spread it into a round, thin shape. Cook until firmed up and golden brown, 2 to 3 minutes, then flip the tortilla and cook the other side for 1 to 2 minutes more. Do not attempt to flip the tortilla before it is well cooked on one side, or it might break apart. Keep warm by wrapping in a kitchen towel while you cook the rest of the batter, regreasing the pan each time.

To serve, divide the tortillas between six plates and top each tortilla with some of the mung bean mixture. Sprinkle with the extra herbs, and serve immediately.

COOK'S NOTE Psyllium husk is a soluble fiber that works very well as a bulking agent in gluten-free goods. It helps support digestion, replacing gums, which are common in gluten-free baking, but can create digestive issues. Alternatively, you can use ground up chia seeds, flax seeds, or a combination.

I wasn't sure I would like coconut milk in a savory risotto, but was I happily surprised at the result. The combination of lemony tang and creamy coconut milk brings a whole new level of flavor and texture to risotto. When you add mushrooms to the mix, it's almost miraculous. If the rice hasn't been soaked overnight, expect the process to take longer and to require more liquid.

LEMONY MUSHROOM RISOTTO

• • •

RISOTTO

1 tablespoon coconut oil

1 large leek, white and light green parts, finely chopped

1 medium yellow onion, finely diced

5 cloves garlic, minced

Sea salt

2 cups short grain brown rice, soaked overnight, rinsed, and drained

2-inch piece of kombu

3 cups vegetable broth, preferably homemade

2½ cups coconut milk

½ cup cilantro, finely chopped

Black pepper

MUSHROOMS

2 tablespoons coconut oil

1½ pounds mushrooms (any kind), coarsely chopped

3 cloves garlic, minced

2 tablespoons lemon juice

½ cup parsley, finely chopped, plus more for garnish

1 teaspoon sea salt

Black pepper

SERVES 4 TO 6

To make the risotto, heat a large sauté pan on medium heat and melt the coconut oil. Add the leek, onion, garlic, and a pinch of salt. Sauté until translucent, stirring occasionally, about 5 minutes. Add the rice and cook, stirring often, until the rice looks pearly, about 5 minutes. Add the kombu. Start adding the broth and the coconut milk, alternating 1 cup at a time. Bring to a boil, then reduce the heat and simmer, stirring often, until the rice is soft, about 45 minutes. Wait until most of the liquid is absorbed before adding more.

About 10 minutes before the rice is done, make the mushrooms. Heat a large sauté pan over medium heat and melt the coconut oil. Add the mushrooms, garlic, and lemon juice. Cook, stirring often, until the mushrooms are soft and cooked, about 5 minutes. Mix in the parsley and salt, and season with black pepper to taste.

When the rice is done, remove the kombu. Mix in 2 teaspoons of salt, the cilantro, and a few grinds of black pepper. Transfer to a serving bowl and top with the mushrooms and extra parsley. Serve immediately.

COOK'S NOTE Kombu is a type of dark-colored kelp, or sea vegetable. Sea vegetables, in general, are rich sources of many minerals, B vitamins, and iodine. Add kombu to sauces, soups, and broths, as well as stews and even cooking water for grains. Find kombu at Asian markets and health food stores.

This simple and flavorful vegan curry feels indulgent and satisfying. Well spiced, with ample amounts of ginger, paprika, cardamom, cinnamon, cayenne, and anti-inflammatory turmeric, it packs a lot of nutritional punch—and makes a great topping for cauliflower "couscous" (see page 78).

SWEET POTATO, SPINACH, AND CHICKPEA CURRY

Heat a Dutch oven over medium heat. Melt the coconut oil and add the cumin seeds. Toast the seeds, stirring often, until fragrant, about 1 minute. Add the onion, garlic, and ginger with a pinch of salt. Cook, stirring occasionally, until the onion is translucent, about 5 minutes. Stir in the turmeric, cayenne, paprika, cardamom, cinnamon, and 2 teaspoons of salt. Add the sweet potato, broth, and coconut milk, and make sure the sweet potatoes are immersed in the liquid by pushing them down with a wooden spoon. Raise the heat to medium-high, and bring to a boil. Reduce the heat and simmer until almost tender, 10 to 15 minutes. Stir in the chickpeas and add black pepper to taste. Add the spinach, in batches if necessary, and allow it to wilt. Do not overcook—keep it on the heat for 2 minutes. Stir in the parsley and serve immediately.

• • •

1 tablespoon coconut oil

1 teaspoon cumin seeds

1 medium onion, diced

4 cloves garlic, minced

1-inch piece fresh ginger, peeled and minced

Sea salt

1 teaspoon ground turmeric

½ teaspoon cayenne pepper

1 teaspoon sweet paprika

½ teaspoon ground cardamom

¼ teaspoon ground cinnamon

1 large sweet potato (about 1½ pounds), peeled and cut into 1-inch cubes

1 cup vegetable broth

1½ cups coconut milk

1 cup cooked chickpeas

Black pepper

1 pound baby spinach

⅓ cup flat-leaf parsley, finely chopped

SERVES 4

· · ·

ZUCCHINI, FENNEL, AND RADISH CARPACCIO 61

COCONUT RICE WITH ALMONDS AND GOLDEN RAISINS 62

SPINACH AND WATERMELON SALAD
WITH BALSAMIC REDUCTION 63

CABBAGE, CARROT, AND JICAMA SLAW IN LETTUCE CUPS 64

COCONUT SESAME NOODLES WITH BABY BOK CHOY
AND TAMARIND DRESSING 67

SHREDDED CABBAGE, CHICKPEA, AND CELERY SALAD 69

CUCUMBER COCONUT SALAD 70

GINGER CREAMED CORN 70

MILLET SANDWICH BREAD 71

CARROT, COCONUT, AND ARAME SALAD 72

SHAVED ZUCCHINI SALAD WITH PISTACHIO DRESSING 74

MASHED PARSNIPS AND CHIVES 75

SHREDDED KALE, JICAMA, AND APPLE SALAD
WITH TOASTED COCONUT 77

CAULIFLOWER "COUSCOUS" WITH TURMERIC
AND GREEN ONION 78

SPAGHETTI SQUASH, SPINACH, AND CHICKPEAS
WITH COCONUT LEMONGRASS 79

ROASTED BUTTERNUT SQUASH AND SWISS CHARD
WITH GREEN COCONUT HARISSA 80

SALADS AND SIDES

· · · · · ·

Too often we think of a salad as just a bowl of greens drizzled with oil and vinegar, and of sides as plates of starch or vegetables. They can seem like an afterthought, meant as an obligatory complement to a main dish, but certainly not the co-star of a meal.

When prepared thoughtfully, salads and sides can truly shine! They can carry all manner of flavor and texture and be just as enticing as the main course. Many of the best sides can also be modified—by adding a little protein, or served in larger portions—to become main courses in their own right.

In this chapter, coconut blends with fresh, clean ingredients. Most of these dishes simply take advantage of readily available in-season whole foods. Coconut meat makes a nourishing addition to many sides and salads, and coconut milk and vinegar mixed together with lime or lemon juice are a terrific go-to base for dressings. Here you'll find dishes ranging from new twists on old classics—Ginger Creamed Corn (page 70) and Coconut Rice with Almonds and Golden Raisins (page 62)—to more adventuresome combinations—Carrot, Coconut, and Arame Salad (page 72) and Roasted Butternut Squash and Swiss Chard with Green Coconut Harissa (page 80). All these recipes are healthy and simple to make, yet intensely flavorful.

This must be the most perfect salad: ridiculously delicious, incredibly festive, and complicated-looking, yet utterly simple to make. A little slicing, a little chopping, a little assembling, and your guests will be wowed. This looks best when assembled on a round platter.

• • •

DRESSING

3 tablespoons olive oil

2 tablespoons coconut vinegar

Zest of 1 lime

Pinch of sea salt

SALAD

1 large zucchini (about 11 ounces), ends trimmed and thinly sliced

1 small fennel bulb (about 4 ounces), thinly sliced

3 or 4 radishes, trimmed and thinly sliced

1/3 cup finely chopped fresh coconut meat

1/4 cup mint, finely chopped

SERVES 4 TO 6

ZUCCHINI, FENNEL, AND RADISH CARPACCIO

To make the dressing, in a small bowl, whisk together the olive oil, coconut vinegar, lime zest, and salt. Set aside.

To make the salad, lay the slices on a round platter in a circular pattern, slightly overlapping both the slices and the layers. Start with the cucumber, then the radishes, then the fennel. Sprinkle the coconut meat, drizzle on the dressing, and finish with the mint. Serve immediately.

I have had coconut rice in many different countries, as it is part of the culinary landscape in the Caribbean, Latin America, and parts of Asia. In this version, toasted almonds and golden raisins bring touches of crunch and sweetness to the dish. This coconut rice beautifully accompanies stews, tagines, roasted chicken, and grilled steak. Add a vegetable dish and side salad to make a complete meal. If using boxed vegetable broth, choose low sodium broth and add less salt than the recipe calls for.

COCONUT RICE WITH ALMONDS AND GOLDEN RAISINS

• • •

2 cups brown rice, soaked overnight, drained, and rinsed

1½ cups coconut milk

1½ cups unsalted vegetable broth, preferably homemade

1½ teaspoons sea salt

⅓ cup almonds, coarsely chopped

¼ cup golden raisins

⅓ cup parsley, coarsely chopped

Black pepper

SERVES 4 TO 6

In a large saucepan or Dutch oven, combine the rice, coconut milk, vegetable broth, and salt. Bring to a boil over medium-high heat, then reduce to low and cook, uncovered, stirring occasionally, until the rice is tender, about 40 minutes.

While the rice is cooking, heat a medium sauté pan over medium heat. Add the almonds to the pan, and toast, stirring continuously, until fragrant and slightly browned, about 3 minutes. Watch closely to make sure they don't to burn, and transfer them immediately to a plate or cutting board to cool.

When the rice is done, stir in the toasted almonds, raisins, and parsley. Season with black pepper to taste. Serve immediately.

In this very refreshing summer salad, the sweetness of the balsamic reduction perfectly complements both the watermelon and the creamy diced coconut meat. With the addition of baby spinach, it feels more like a meal and less like a simple fruit salad. Save any leftover balsamic reduction for other creations—try it on grilled peaches or figs wrapped in prosciutto.

SPINACH AND WATERMELON SALAD WITH BALSAMIC REDUCTION

• • •

½ cup balsamic vinegar

6 ounces baby spinach

3 cups small-diced watermelon

1½ cups diced fresh coconut meat

½ cup mint, roughly chopped

2 tablespoons olive oil

2 pinches fleur de sel or sea salt

Black pepper

⅓ cup pumpkin seeds, toasted (see Cook's Note page 16)

SERVES 4 TO 6

In a small saucepan, bring the vinegar to a boil over medium heat. Reduce the heat and simmer, uncovered, until the vinegar has reduced by about two-thirds and is thick enough to coat a spoon, 8 to 10 minutes. Set aside to cool.

In a large salad bowl, combine the spinach, and three-quarters each of the watermelon, coconut, and mint. Add the olive oil and fleur de sel, season with black pepper to taste, and toss. Top with the remaining quarter of the watermelon, coconut, and mint and drizzle with 1 to 2 tablespoons of the balsamic reduction, to taste. Sprinkle over the pumpkin seeds and serve.

When the weather is warm and we need refreshing foods to cool us down, this veggie slaw in lettuce cups certainly fits the bill. It would be easy to turn it into a main dish by adding some tempeh or grilled fish or chicken. To save time, grate and shred the carrots, jicama, and cabbage in a food processor fitted with a grating and shredding disk.

CABBAGE, CARROT, AND JICAMA SLAW IN LETTUCE CUPS

To make the slaw, in a large bowl, mix together the carrots, jicama, cabbage, mango, red onion, coconut meat, mint, sesame seeds, and salt.

To make the dressing, combine the olive oil, coconut milk, vinegar, aminos, lime zest, chile powder, and salt in a blender. Process on high until smooth, about 30 seconds. Drizzle onto the vegetable mixture and mix well.

Fill the butter lettuce leaves with about 1/3 cup of the mixture and sprinkle each with a bit of extra chopped mint and sesame seeds. Serve immediately.

• • •

SLAW

2 large carrots, grated

1 small jicama (about 12 ounces), finely grated

1/2 small red cabbage (about 6 ounces), shredded

1 mango, finely chopped

1/4 red onion, finely diced

1 1/2 cups chopped fresh coconut meat

1/4 cup mint, finely chopped, plus more for garnish

1 tablespoon sesame seeds, plus more for garnish

1/2 teaspoon sea salt

DRESSING

1/4 cup olive oil

1/4 cup coconut milk

3 tablespoons coconut vinegar

1 tablespoon coconut aminos

Lime zest from 2 limes

1/4 teaspoon chile powder

1/2 teaspoon sea salt

Butter lettuce leaves, for serving

SERVES 4 TO 6

• • •

1½ pounds fresh coconut meat

1 baby bok choy, coarsely chopped

2 yellow bell peppers, seeded, deribbed, and julienned

2 green onions, white and green parts, finely chopped

½ cup cilantro, finely chopped

½ cup mint, finely chopped

DRESSING

2 cloves garlic, minced

1 tablespoon tahini

1 tablespoon coconut aminos

2-inch piece fresh ginger, peeled and minced

½ small jalapeño, seeded and finely minced (optional)

½ teaspoon tamarind paste

3 tablespoons olive oil

¼ cup lime juice

½ teaspoon coconut nectar

1¼ teaspoon sea salt

2 tablespoons sesame seeds, for garnish

SERVES 4 TO 6

Finely sliced strips of coconut meat can easily replace glutinous grain noodles—and feel just as satisfying. Here, coconut "noodles" are mixed with baby bok choy and yellow peppers and drizzled with a tangy tamarind and jalapeño dressing. This flavor-packed recipe is super healthy but still feels indulgent.

COCONUT SESAME NOODLES WITH BABY BOK CHOY AND TAMARIND DRESSING

To prepare the noodles, slice the coconut meat into thin, noodle-like, strips with a very sharp knife. Combine the coconut, bok choy, bell peppers, green onions, cilantro, and mint in a large bowl.

To make the dressing, whisk together all of the ingredients. Drizzle the dressing onto the salad and mix well. Sprinkle on the sesame seeds and serve immediately.

DRESSING

¼ cup olive oil

3 tablespoons lime juice

2 tablespoons coconut vinegar

3 teaspoons Dijon mustard

¼ head red cabbage, cored and very thinly sliced

¼ head green cabbage, cored and very thinly sliced

1½ cups cooked chickpeas

2 stalks celery, very thinly sliced

¾ cup dried shredded coconut

⅓ cup sunflower seeds

¼ cup hemp seeds

¼ cup dill, finely chopped, plus extra for garnish

3 generous pinches sea salt

Black pepper

SERVES 4 TO 6

Part of the huge family of cruciferous vegetables, cabbage contains many anti-inflammatory compounds and antioxidants, which can help protect the body's immune system, warding off disease. This salad is refreshing, very tasty, and dead simple to create, especially if you use a mandoline to slice up the cabbage and celery.

SHREDDED CABBAGE, CHICKPEA, AND CELERY SALAD

For the dressing, whisk together the oil, lime juice, vinegar, and mustard. Set aside.

In a large salad bowl, mix together the red cabbage, green cabbage, chickpeas, celery, coconut, sunflower seeds, hemp seeds, dill, and salt. Season with black pepper to taste. Drizzle on the dressing and toss well. Garnish with the extra dill and serve immediately.

• • •

2 large cucumbers,
ends trimmed, cut in
half lengthwise and
thinly sliced

1/2 red onion, thinly sliced

1 1/2 cups coconut meat,
diced

3 tablespoons olive oil

2 tablespoons coconut
vinegar

1 teaspoon coconut nectar

1/2 teaspoon sea salt

1/4 cup dill, finely chopped

SERVES 4 TO 6

This salad makes a perfectly refreshing summer side when it is too hot to move, let alone cook. Requiring very few ingredients, it comes together in a snap.

CUCUMBER COCONUT SALAD

Mix the cucumbers, onion, and coconut meat in a large bowl.

In a small bowl, whisk together the olive oil, vinegar, coconut nectar, and salt.

Add the dressing to the salad, sprinkle on the dill, and mix well. Serve immediately.

• • •

8 cups corn kernels,
fresh or frozen, thawed

1/2 large red onion, finely
diced

2 cups coconut milk

2 tablespoons lime juice

2-inch piece fresh ginger,
peeled and minced

1 teaspoon sea salt

Black pepper

1/3 cup cilantro, finely
chopped

SERVES 4 TO 6

Who knew that coconut milk would taste so divine as a base for creamed corn? It is delightful, and even more so with a touch of freshly minced ginger and cilantro. You may never go back to the more traditional version made with dairy cream.

GINGER CREAMED CORN

Combine the corn, red onion, coconut milk, lime juice, and ginger in a large sauté pan over medium-high heat. Bring to a boil, then reduce the heat, and simmer gently until most of the liquid has been absorbed, 8 to 10 minutes. Add the salt and season with black pepper to taste. Sprinkle on the cilantro. Serve immediately as a side dish with grilled fish, meat, or tempeh.

Millet flour adds a nuttiness to this gluten-free bread, which works beautifully in both savory and sweet uses. It's brilliant as a sandwich bread—try it with coconut aioli (see page 49), lettuce, heirloom tomatoes, avocado, and microgreens—and it's also great toasted, for breakfast or a snack. Although it tastes best right out of the oven, it will keep, refrigerated, for a few days; just toast it before enjoying again.

MILLET SANDWICH BREAD

• • •

Coconut oil

1¼ cups almond flour

¾ cup millet flour

3 tablespoons coconut flour

¼ cup arrowroot starch

3 tablespoons psyllium husk (see Cook's Note, page 53)

1 teaspoon baking soda

1 teaspoon sea salt

1 cup coconut milk

3 eggs

½ cup chopped fresh coconut meat

2 tablespoons coconut nectar

1 tablespoon coconut vinegar

⅓ cup coconut butter, melted

MAKES ONE 8½ BY 4½-INCH LOAF

Preheat the oven to 350°F. Line the bottom of a 8½ by 4½-inch bread pan with unbleached parchment paper. Grease the sides with coconut oil.

In a large mixing bowl, whisk together the almond flour, millet flour, coconut flour, arrowroot, psyllium husk, baking soda, and sea salt. Combine the coconut milk, eggs, and coconut meat, nectar, vinegar, and butter in a high speed blender. Blend on high for a few seconds, until smooth. Add the wet ingredients to the dry ingredients and mix well.

Pour the batter into the prepared bread pan. Bake until golden brown on the top and a toothpick inserted in the center comes out clean, 45 to 50 minutes. Slide a knife along the edges of the pan. Transfer the bread to a cutting board and allow to cool for about 10 minutes before slicing. It's best served right away, but can be stored in the refrigerator for up to 5 days. After it's a day or so old, slice and toast before serving.

Whenever possible, I try to include sea vegetables such as arame in my cooking; find it in well-stocked grocery stores or health food stores. Sea vegetables provide many nutrients that we are often deficient in, including a range of minerals and thyroid-supportive iodine. With its citrusy notes and bright coloring, this salad has become a little bit of an obsession in my home, and I trust that you will find yourself making it over and over again. It's easiest to grate the carrots in a food processor fitted with a fine grating wheel.

CARROT, COCONUT, AND ARAME SALAD

For the dressing, whisk together the olive oil, coconut milk, lime juice, and salt in a small bowl. Set aside.

In a large bowl, mix together the carrots, arame, coconut, red onion, and cilantro. Drizzle on the dressing and toss well. Serve immediately.

• • •

DRESSING

3 tablespoons olive oil

3 tablespoons coconut milk

5 tablespoons lime juice

¾ teaspoon sea salt

5 large carrots (about 2 pounds), ends trimmed and finely grated

⅓ cup arame, soaked in warm water for 5 minutes, drained, and coarsely chopped

½ cup unsweetened coconut, shredded

½ medium red onion, diced

¼ cup cilantro, finely chopped

SERVES 4 TO 6

...

2/3 cup coconut milk

1/2 cup pistachios, toasted
(see Cook's Note, page 16)

1/2 cup flat-leaf parsley,
roughly chopped, plus
more for garnish

2 cloves garlic

2 tablespoons olive oil

1/4 cup lemon juice

1 1/4 teaspoons sea salt

Black pepper

5 large zucchini (about
3 pounds), ends trimmed,
seeds removed, and peeled
into long strands

1/2 cup pine nuts, toasted
(see Cook's Note, page 16)

SERVES 4 TO 6

Salads can be created from all sorts of cooked and raw vegetables. Here, raw zucchini is shaved into thin strips and flavored with an herb and pistachio dressing. This salad can serve as a side dish or even as a main meal with the addition of roasted chicken, grilled fish, or sautéed tempeh.

SHAVED ZUCCHINI SALAD WITH PISTACHIO DRESSING

In a high-speed blender, combine the coconut milk, pistachios, parsley, garlic, olive oil, lemon juice, and salt. Season with black pepper to taste. Process on high until smooth, about 1 minute. Drizzle the dressing onto the zucchini in a large bowl and mix well. Sprinkle over the pine nuts and extra parsley and serve.

···

1 tablespoon coconut oil

1 yellow onion, finely diced

2-inch piece fresh ginger, peeled and minced

2 cloves garlic, minced

Sea salt

1/2 teaspoon cumin seeds

1/4 teaspoon grated nutmeg

5 or 6 parsnips (about 4 pounds), peeled and finely diced

2 1/2 cups coconut milk

2 tablespoons coconut butter

3 tablespoons finely chopped chives, plus more for garnish

SERVES 4 TO 6

Looking for an alternative to mashed potatoes? Parsnips look like large white carrots but have a sweet, sharp flavor all their own. Mashed with coconut milk and coconut butter, they make a luxe cold-weather side dish that would be a wonderful addition to any Thanksgiving table.

MASHED PARSNIPS AND CHIVES

Heat a large pot or Dutch oven over medium heat. Melt the coconut oil, then add the onion, ginger, garlic, and a pinch of salt. Cook, stirring often, until the onion is translucent, about 5 minutes. Stir in the cumin and nutmeg. Add the parsnips and coconut milk and bring to a boil. Reduce the heat to medium, cover, and cook, stirring often, until tender, 8 to 10 minutes.

Using an immersion blender or a potato masher, purée the parsnips until smooth, adding a touch of water if the mixture appears too dry. Mix in the coconut butter, 2 teaspoons of salt, and the chives. Serve immediately, garnished with the extra chives.

Raw kale leaves can be tough and unpleasant to eat, but shredding them very finely can turn them into a very palatable salad. The addition of sweet grated jicama and sliced apple softens the strong and slightly bitter taste of the kale and balances all the flavors beautifully.

SHREDDED KALE, JICAMA, AND APPLE SALAD WITH TOASTED COCONUT

• • •

1 cup coconut flakes

1 tablespoon coconut oil, melted

1/4 teaspoon fleur de sel or sea salt

DRESSING

3 tablespoons olive oil

2 tablespoons coconut milk

4 tablespoons lemon juice

1/2 teaspoon sea salt

2 bunches lacinato kale (about 1 pound), stemmed and julienned (see Cook's Note, page 80)

1 medium jicama (about 1 1/4 pounds), ends trimmed, peeled, and grated

1 crisp apple, quartered, cored, and thinly sliced

1/2 cup walnuts, toasted (see Cook's Note, page 16), coarsely chopped

SERVES 4 TO 6

Preheat the oven to 350°F. Line a baking sheet with unbleached parchment paper.

Put the coconut flakes in a medium bowl, drizzle with the coconut oil, and mix well.

Lay the coconut flakes on the prepared baking sheet and sprinkle with the fleur de sel. Bake until golden brown, 6 to 8 minutes. Watch carefully to keep from burning. Remove to a plate lined with paper towels to cool.

To make the dressing, in a bowl, whisk together the olive oil, coconut milk, lemon juice, and salt. Set aside.

Mix the kale, jicama, and apple slices in a large bowl. Add the dressing to the salad and mix well. Serve immediately topped with the toasted coconut and walnuts.

This is the perfect side dish to complement stews, tagines, grilled meat or tempeh, or even poached eggs and bacon in the morning. Cauliflower "couscous" has the texture of a grain with the nutritional goodness of health-supportive vegetables. And when it is cooked with coconut milk instead of the usual water, it boasts even more nutritional value and flavor.

CAULIFLOWER "COUSCOUS" WITH TURMERIC AND GREEN ONION

• • •

1 head cauliflower
(2½ pounds), leaves
and stalk removed,
cut into 1-inch chunks

2 tablespoons coconut oil

¼ cup coconut milk

½ teaspoon ground
turmeric

1 teaspoon sea salt

1 green onion, white and
green parts, finely chopped

½ cup flat-leaf parsley,
finely chopped

Black pepper

SERVES 4 TO 6

In a food processor, pulse the cauliflower 10 to 15 times, until it has the appearance of rice or couscous.

Heat a large sauté pan over medium heat. Melt the coconut oil and add the cauliflower, coconut milk, turmeric, and salt. Sauté, stirring often, until soft but still al dente, about 5 minutes. Mix in the green onion and parsley. Season with black pepper to taste.

Serve immediately. This will keep, refrigerated, for 3 to 4 days. Simply reheat on the stovetop with a little broth or water.

1 medium spaghetti squash
(about 5 pounds), halved
and seeded

SAUCE

1¼ cups coconut milk

2 lemongrass sticks, cut
into 2-inch pieces and
bruised with a mallet

2-inch piece fresh ginger,
peeled and minced

1 clove garlic, minced

1 teaspoon minced
jalapeño (optional)

1 tablespoon coconut
aminos

1 teaspoon coconut vinegar

1 tablespoon lime juice

2 teaspoons sea salt

Black pepper

3 cups baby spinach

1 red pepper, seeded and
coarsely chopped

1½ cups cooked chickpeas

½ cup coarsely chopped
cilantro, plus extra for
garnish

3 tablespoons minced
chives, plus extra for
garnish

SERVES 4 TO 6

Tangy lemongrass and lime are natural taste builders for
any dish that uses coconut milk. And what a welcome
combination it is, since coconut milk will not curdle like dairy
milk when it comes into contact with lime juice. This sauce
will taste very salty, but will be fine once it is mixed into the
unsalted squash.

SPAGHETTI SQUASH, SPINACH, AND CHICKPEAS WITH COCONUT LEMONGRASS

Preheat the oven to 400°F. Line a large baking sheet with
unbleached parchment paper.

Lay the squash face down on the prepared baking sheet. Bake until
soft, about 45 minutes.

Meanwhile, make the sauce. In a medium saucepan over medium
heat, combine the coconut milk, lemongrass, ginger, and garlic
and bring to a boil. Reduce the heat to low and simmer, uncovered,
until thickened and reduced by about a third, 12 to 15 minutes.
Remove the lemongrass and add the jalapeño, coconut aminos,
coconut vinegar, lime juice, and salt and season with black pepper
to taste. Keep warm.

Combine the spinach, pepper, and chickpeas in a large serving bowl.

When the squash is cooked, turn it over and scrape the inside with
a fork, producing spaghetti-like strands. Transfer to the serving
bowl, allowing the heat of the squash to warm the spinach, pepper,
and chickpeas, about 3 minutes. Stir in the sauce, cilantro, and
chives. Top with the extra chives and cilantro and serve immediately.

• • •

1 butternut squash (about
4 pounds), peeled, seeded,
and chopped in to bite-
sized pieces

1 tablespoon coconut oil,
melted

Sea salt and black pepper

HARISSA

1½ cups coarsely chopped
fresh coconut meat

1 cup coconut milk

1 large jalapeño pepper,
stemmed and coarsely
chopped

½ cup parsley leaves

3 cloves garlic

Zest of 1 lime

Juice of 1 lime

1 teaspoon cumin seeds,
toasted (see Cook's Note,
page 16)

1 teaspoon coriander seeds,
toasted

2 teaspoons sea salt

Black pepper

3 cups Swiss chard,
julienned (see Cook's Notes)

1-inch piece fresh ginger,
peeled and minced

½ cup walnuts, toasted
and coarsely chopped

1 pomegranate, seeded
(see Cook's Note, page 16)

SERVES 4 TO 6

Harissa is a spicy North African chile paste used to increase
flavor and heat in many traditional dishes. Typically red, this
recipe yields a green version made with jalapeño peppers.

ROASTED BUTTERNUT SQUASH
AND SWISS CHARD WITH GREEN
COCONUT HARISSA

Preheat the oven to 400°F. Line a baking sheet with unbleached
parchment paper.

Place the squash on the baking sheet. Drizzle the coconut oil and
toss. Sprinkle with a generous amount of salt and black pepper
and bake until very soft, 30 to 40 minutes, depending on the size.

While the squash is baking, prepare the harissa. Combine the coconut
meat, coconut milk, jalapeño, parsley, garlic, lime zest, lime juice,
cumin, coriander, salt, and a few grinds of black pepper in the bowl
of a food processor. Process on high until puréed, about 1 minute.
Set aside.

Add the chard and ginger to a large bowl. When the squash is
cooked, transfer it to the bowl and allow the heat of the squash to
wilt the chard for about 3 minutes, then mix well. Top with walnuts
and pomegranate seeds and serve immediately with the coconut
harissa on the side.

🥄 **COOK'S NOTE** To julienne Swiss chard and kale, slice out the
center vein of each leaf, then stack the leaves and roll them together
before slicing them very finely widthwise.

TRAIL MIX 85

CRAZY-SIMPLE CHARD CHIPS 86

HERBED COCONUT HUMMUS 89

CHEESY PAPRIKA POPCORN 90

SPICY COCONUT CHIPS 91

SNACKS

. . . .

It is perfectly civilized to have, once in a while, a crunchy, sweet, or salty snack that bridges the gap between meals or simply makes movie watching a little more enjoyable. Coconut makes the perfect addition to many different kinds of snacks, claiming a permanent place in my house's snack repertoire.

I didn't think my son (a picky eater) would eat chard chips (page 86), since he won't eat fresh chard, but he actually loves them—I can't make chard chips fast enough for him to eat. Coconut chips (page 91) make great snacks, too—so simple to make, yet very nourishing and highly addictive. In the same dry-crunchy category is my trail mix (page 85), which has seaweed added for an extra nutritional boost, and paprika popcorn (page 90), with just the right amount of spice. Or, for something a little more dippy, coconut perfectly transforms hummus (page 89) into the creamiest, most satisfying dip for raw vegetables or pita.

Low in sweeteners and high in fiber, protein, and flavor, this trail mix is very sustaining. Adding chopped nori to the mix takes the nutrition of this snack up another notch. Nori is a sea vegetable most commonly used in sushi. It's rich in minerals, including iodine and other nutrients, and can be purchased online or from any well-stocked grocery store.

TRAIL MIX

1 tablespoon coconut oil

1 tablespoon coconut nectar

2 tablespoons sesame seeds

½ cup almonds, coarsely chopped

½ cup pecans, coarsely chopped

½ cup coconut flakes

⅓ cup pumpkin seeds

⅓ cup golden raisins, dried cranberries, or other dried fruit

⅓ cup finely chopped nori

¼ teaspoon sea salt

MAKES ABOUT 3 CUPS

Preheat the oven to 350°F. Line a baking sheet with unbleached parchment paper.

In a small saucepan over low heat, gently melt the coconut oil. Whisk in the coconut nectar.

Combine the sesame seeds, almonds, pecans, coconut flakes, pumpkin seeds, raisins, nori, and salt in a large bowl and mix well.

Lay the mixture on the prepared baking sheet and spread it out evenly. Roast until fragrant, about 10 minutes. Watch carefully and make sure the coconut flakes do not burn. Allow to cool completely before serving or storing. Trail mix will keep at room temperature for 2 weeks.

The first time I made chard chips, my son wanted to know what they tasted like before even trying them. "They are like kale chips, but better, not as bitter," I explained. A little suspicious, he still tried one, and ended up gobbling up the whole bowl. Now, chard chips have replaced kale chips in our house.

CRAZY-SIMPLE CHARD CHIPS

Preheat the oven to 300°F. Line two large baking sheets with unbleached parchment paper.

Remove the center stems of the chard leaves. Stack the leaves together, roll them, and chop them into bite-sized pieces. Add to a large bowl. Mix in the coconut oil. Sprinkle with the fleur de sel and mix well.

Arrange the chard on the baking sheets; do not overcrowd. (You will need to bake in two batches.) Bake until wilted and crispy, 30 to 35 minutes. If some chips are still soggy, put them back into the oven until they crisp up, about 5 minutes. Allow to cool completely. Serve immediately.

• • •

2 bunches Swiss chard (about 1½ pounds)

1 tablespoon coconut oil, melted

½ teaspoon fleur de sel or sea salt

MAKES A MEDIUM BOWL

I should have guessed that adding fresh coconut meat to hummus would give it a silky smooth, creamy finish that really complements the traditional hummus ingredients of chickpeas, garlic, and citrus. But I had never tried it until I started writing this book, and I was very pleasantly surprised at the results. Try it!

HERBED COCONUT HUMMUS

Place the chickpeas in a medium saucepan with enough water to cover by 1 inch. Bring to a boil over high heat, then reduce the heat to low and simmer, covered, until the chickpeas are tender, about 35 minutes. Pour into a fine-mesh sieve to drain.

Place the chickpeas in the bowl of a food processor. Add the cilantro, coconut meat, ginger, garlic, tahini, olive oil, lime juice, coconut aminos, sea salt, and a few grinds of black pepper. Process until puréed and smooth, about 1 minute. Taste and add more aminos, if needed. Serve immediately with vegetables, crackers, or bread.

• • •

½ cup dried chickpeas, soaked overnight, drained, and rinsed

¼ cup cilantro leaves

½ cup chopped fresh coconut meat

1-inch piece fresh ginger, peeled and minced

2 large cloves garlic

2 tablespoons tahini

¾ cup olive oil

¼ cup lime juice

3 teaspoons coconut aminos

2 teaspoons sea salt

Black pepper

Sliced vegetables, crackers, or bread for serving

MAKES ABOUT 2 CUPS

Ah, the tasty crunch of a freshly popped bowl of organic popcorn! So easy to make, and free of the toxic ingredients that plague microwavable popcorn. To prevent burning, use a large saucepan or an old fashioned stovetop popper (available online) with a turning handle.

CHEESY PAPRIKA POPCORN

. . .

½ cup popcorn kernels

3 tablespoons coconut oil

1½ teaspoons sea salt

3 tablespoons nutritional yeast

1 teaspoon paprika

MAKES A LARGE BOWL

Combine the popcorn, coconut oil, and salt in a large saucepan. Cover, and turn the heat to medium. Holding the lid down with an oven mitt, shake the pan back and forth continuously above the flame. Popping will start within 4 or 5 minutes. Once the popping has slowed so that there is 1 second between pops, turn off the heat.

Pour the popcorn into a large bowl. Sprinkle on the nutritional yeast and paprika and mix well. Taste and add more salt if desired. Serve immediately.

Crunchy, salty, spicy, and really healthy, these chips might just be the perfect snack. And they only take a few minutes to make. Feel free to double the recipe—if you don't, you will wish you had.

SPICY COCONUT CHIPS

• • •

4 cups unsweetened coconut flakes

2 tablespoons coconut oil, melted

1 tablespoon lime juice

¾ teaspoon fleur de sel or sea salt

½ teaspoon hot paprika

MAKES ABOUT 4 CUPS

Preheat the oven to 350°F. Line a large baking sheet with unbleached parchment paper.

Put the coconut flakes in a medium bowl and mix in the coconut oil and lime juice. Sprinkle over the fleur de sel and paprika and mix well. Spread the coconut on the prepared baking sheet and bake until golden brown, 6 to 8 minutes. Watch carefully toward the end so they don't burn. Transfer them immediately to a plate lined with paper towels to cool completely. They will crisp up as they cool. Serve immediately, or store in an air-tight container for about a day.

· · ·

BLUEBERRY KEFIR 95

COCONUT LIMEADE 96

POMEGRANATE MINT SHRUB 96

CREAMY ROOIBOS CHAI 97

SPICED HOT CHOCOLATE 98

DRINKS

· · · · · · ·

You are probably familiar with coconut water (aka the athlete's replenisher) or with coconut milk added to smoothies for extra creaminess and flavor. But what about fermented coconut drinks, such as a coconut kefir flavored with sweet blueberries (page 95), or a sparkling Pomegranate Mint Shrub (page 96) that might possibly be one of the most refreshing and festive summer drinks ever? You could also try something more exotic, like creamy Coconut Limeade (page 96) from my husband's home country of Colombia, reworked to include healthier ingredients and less sugar. Or, if it's winter and it's cold outside, try a warm and decaffeinated (but very energizing) rooibos chai made from red tea spiced with cardamom, allspice, cinnamon, cloves, ginger, and nutmeg (page 97). It's a feast for the senses that will warm you all over. Or try hot chocolate spiked with cinnamon and a touch of cayenne (page 98)—you will be wowed by its richness and complex flavor.

There are so many ways to incorporate coconut into drinks—its versatility is inspiring. And with coconut's nutritional properties, these drinks are not just pleasurable, but healthy, too. Next time you're making a smoothie, a cozy warm drink, or even a summer refresher, don't forget the coconut!

Kefir is a cultured drink that is rich in beneficial bacteria that support our immune and digestive systems. It can be made from milk or water. Water kefir looks like cloudy water, and tastes like a sparkling, slightly sweet, cultured drink. Milk kefir has an opaque white color and a thicker texture, like a smoothie; it tastes a little like liquid yogurt, but more sour. Milk kefir and yogurt are quite different from one another, though. Yogurt bacteria keep the digestive tract clean and feed beneficial bacteria, whereas kefir bacteria colonize the digestive tract with different bacterial strains and yeasts.

• • •

3 cups coconut milk

2 cups coconut water

¼ cup coconut water kefir

3 cups blueberries

Seeds from 2 vanilla beans, or 1 tablespoon vanilla extract

MAKES ABOUT 6 CUPS

Kefir is traditionally made by mixing milk or water with kefir grains or powdered kefir starter. If you are vegan, be aware that kefir grains are not completely dairy-free (though they contain minimal dairy, and the lactose, unlike the casein, is usually digested during the culturing process).

For a completely dairy-free version, make coconut milk kefir from coconut milk and coconut water fermented with coconut water kefir. Coconut water kefir can be purchased in well-stocked grocery stores or health food stores, in the refrigerated section. Always make the kefir in a glass jar and stir it with a wooden spoon, as it does not react well to metal.

BLUEBERRY KEFIR

In a large glass jar, combine the coconut milk, coconut water, and coconut water kefir. Mix well with a wooden spoon. Cover loosely with a thin cloth or coffee filter and allow to culture at room temperature until thickened, about 24 hours.

Combine the kefir, blueberries, and vanilla in a high speed blender. Blend on high until smooth, about 30 seconds. Serve immediately or refrigerate for later use. Kefir will keep for about a week.

• • •

2 cups coconut milk

2 cups ice, plus more
for serving

1 cup packed mint leaves

½ cup lime juice

¼ cup coconut nectar

SERVES 4

I tasted my first coconut limeade in my husband Ricardo's home country of Colombia. Nearly every restaurant there offers it, though their versions involve canned coconut cream and a large amount of sugar. I've reworked it here to include healthier ingredients and less sweetener, and also added mint, to make it taste like a creamy mojito. If you are feeling festive, spike this baby with a little rum.

COCONUT LIMEADE

Combine all the ingredients in a high-speed blender. Blend on high until smooth, about 1 minute. Serve immediately over ice.

• • •

4 cups sparkling water

¼ cup pomegranate juice

4 teaspoons coconut
vinegar

1 teaspoon minced fresh
ginger

A handful of mint leaves

2 teaspoons coconut
nectar (optional)

Chopped fresh fruit

Ice

SERVES 4

The shrub is the new "it" drink—a blend of sparkling water, fruit juice, vinegar, and various herbs and fruits. Very refreshing during the summer—or any time plain water feels too boring—it can contain an endless variety of flavors.

POMEGRANATE MINT SHRUB

Combine the sparkling water, juice, coconut vinegar, ginger, mint, coconut nectar, and fruit in a large mason jar or glass pitcher. Crush the mint leaves and fruit to release their juices and stir well to blend in the coconut nectar.

Add plenty of ice and serve immediately.

Chai is an Indian blend of black tea and spices such as cardamom, allspice, cinnamon, cloves, ginger, and nutmeg. This recipe uses rooibos tea, a red tea that is made from the rooibos shrub and is known for its many health properties: it contains numerous minerals and antioxidants, helps support the digestive and cardiovascular systems, and may even help prevent cancer. Spicy and creamy yet completely dairy- and caffeine-free, this coconut chai is the perfect cup of healthy comfort on a cold day.

CREAMY ROOIBOS CHAI

- - -

3 cups water

2 tablespoons loose leaf rooibos tea or 2 rooibos tea bags

½ teaspoon decorticated cardamom (see Cook's Note)

6 cloves

1½ cups coconut milk

2-inch piece fresh ginger, minced

2 teaspoons ground cinnamon, plus more for garnish

Seeds from 2 vanilla beans, or 1 tablespoon vanilla extract

3 tablespoons coconut palm sugar

SERVES 4

Bring the water to a boil in a medium saucepan. Turn off the heat, add the tea, and allow to steep for 10 minutes. Strain out the tea or remove the tea bags.

In a coffee grinder reserved for spices, grind the cardamom and cloves to a powder.

Combine the freshly ground spices, coconut milk, ginger, cinnamon, vanilla, and coconut sugar in a medium saucepan. Bring to a simmer over medium heat, whisking continuously. Using a fine-mesh sieve, strain the coconut milk mixture into the tea and whisk to combine.

Serve immediately with extra cinnamon as a garnish.

COOK'S NOTE Decorticated cardamom, or cardamom seeds, are simply the cardamom seeds that have been removed from their pod. You can do this yourself, by breaking up the pods with your fingers and removing the seeds, or you can purchase already decorticated cardamom in the spice section of your grocery store.

This is a very thick, rich, and deeply satisfying hot chocolate for sipping. A little goes a long way, and a few sips are usually enough, which is why the recipe yields only a cup and a half for four servings. Feel free to double the recipe if you would like a more substantial serving.

SPICED HOT CHOCOLATE

• • •

3½ ounces dark chocolate, chopped

1 cup coconut milk

½ cup coconut water

1 tablespoon coconut sugar

1 teaspoon ground cinnamon

½ teaspoon cayenne pepper

Orange-vanilla whipped cream (page 28), for garnish

SERVES 4

Gently melt the chocolate in a double boiler. Set aside.

Combine the coconut milk, coconut water, and coconut sugar in a medium saucepan. Bring to a low simmer, whisking continuously. Whisk in the melted chocolate, cinnamon, and cayenne. Serve immediately in small cups, topped with a little coconut whipped cream.

· · ·

VANILLA ROSEMARY CRÈME BRÛLÉE 102

COCONUT ORANGE COOKIES 105

STRAWBERRY BASIL ICE CREAM WITH PECAN CRUNCH 106

KIWI COCONUT PANNA COTTA WITH
CARAMELIZED PECANS 107

DATE AND ALMOND TRUFFLES 108

BLACK RICE MANGO SUSHI 110

ALMOND VANILLA CHIA PUDDING
WITH ROASTED BLUEBERRIES 113

DESSERTS

Does anything conjure up more fond memories than the homemade desserts we grew up with? Creamy, fluffy whipped cream hugging summer berries, their juices running down our fingers and chins, eaten in the evening light with crickets chirping in the sticky heat. Or perfectly caramelized crème brûlée (one of my French family's favorite treats), crunchy and smoky on the outside, creamy and soothing on the inside. Or best of all, a summer peach pie with a great-aunt's traditional crust.

In my quest to work with more coconut ingredients in my kitchen, I decided to revisit many of the recipes from my childhood, removing the dairy that they were traditionally made with and replacing it with coconut. I wondered if the recipes would work as well. I quickly realized with delight that the dairy-free versions I created were just as flavorful as the ones I remembered, and sometimes more so.

Used in desserts, coconut shines brightly. A natural element in sweet creations, try it in ice cream (page 106), panna cotta (page 107), or any other sweet treat that would normally contain dairy. Its cream, butter, sugar, oil, and milk all take the place of their dairy counterparts with a few adjustments; and, unlike certain nut milks and nut creams, coconut milk and cream can withstand high temperatures without curdling, which makes them forgiving ingredients in the kitchen.

Plain vanilla crème brûlée already feels like such perfection that it hardly needs any adornment. That is, until you try it with a little rosemary and a pinch of fleur de sel. Oh, my. It takes the flavor and satisfaction to a whole new level.

I created this recipe in honor of my dad, whose all-time favorite dessert is crème brûlée. I wanted to prove to him that this classic could be made dairy-free and remain equally flavorful. Crème brûlée is usually a light ivory color, but it requires white sugar to achieve this result, so I am not keen on it. I don't mind the darker, more golden color that coconut palm sugar gives this version, especially since it is more complex in flavor. I would have liked to use coconut sugar for the crackly sugar topping, as well, but it just burns without caramelizing, so cane sugar is used in its place.

VANILLA ROSEMARY CRÈME BRÛLÉE

Preheat the oven to 350°F.

In a small saucepan over medium-low heat, gently heat the coconut milk until hot but not boiling. Whisk in the vanilla and ¼ teaspoon rosemary. Set aside to cool slightly.

Combine the egg yolks and coconut palm sugar in a large bowl and, using a hand mixer (or a stand mixer fitted with the whisk attachment) on low speed, whip for a few seconds until well incorporated. Pour the coconut milk mixture into the egg yolk mixture and whip again until fully incorporated.

Arrange six 4½-ounce ramekins in a large baking dish. Divide the cream into the ramekins and fill the baking dish with hot water until it reaches halfway up the sides of the ramekins. Bake until set,

• • •

2 cups coconut milk

Seeds from 1 to 2 vanilla beans, or 1 tablespoon vanilla extract

1 teaspoon finely chopped fresh rosemary

5 egg yolks

⅓ cup coconut palm sugar

Cane sugar

¾ teaspoon fleur de sel (see Cook's Note)

SERVES 6

about 30 to 35 minutes. Remove from the oven and refrigerate until cold, at least 2 hours.

Right before serving, sprinkle a light dusting of cane sugar on top of each custard. Using a kitchen torch, gently caramelize the sugar until it is dark brown but not burnt (see Cook's Note). Allow to cool for a couple of minutes and sprinkle on the remaining rosemary and the fleur de sel. Serve immediately.

COOK'S NOTE Small propane torches can be purchased in most kitchen supply stores. Alternatively, the sugar topping can be caramelized under an oven's broiler. Just keep a close eye on it so it doesn't burn, and turn the ramekins a couple of times to even out the color.

Fleur de sel is the fine, uppermost layer of hand-harvested sea salt, traditionally from France's Brittany coast. It has a very refined flavor, and can be found in well-stocked grocery stores or online. Feel free to substitute other good flaky sea salt such as Maldon.

These cookies are to die for—or so say those of my friends and family who have tried them. Grain-free, chewy with coconut, and with just a hint of orange and sea salt—I am addicted to them, and I think you will be as well.

COCONUT ORANGE COOKIES

2 cups almond flour

½ cup unsweetened shredded coconut

2 tablespoons coconut flour

2 tablespoons coconut palm sugar

1 tablespoon arrowroot starch

½ teaspoon baking soda

¼ teaspoon sea salt

¼ cup coconut oil

¼ cup coconut butter

⅓ cup coconut nectar

2 teaspoons vanilla extract

Zest of 1 large orange

1 tablespoon sesame seeds

MAKES ABOUT 2 DOZEN

Preheat the oven to 350°F. Line two large baking sheets with unbleached parchment paper.

In a large bowl, whisk together the almond flour, shredded coconut, coconut flour, coconut sugar, arrowroot, baking soda, and salt.

Combine the coconut oil and coconut butter in a small saucepan over low heat. Gently melt them, then whisk in the coconut sugar, vanilla, and orange zest. Pour into the bowl with the dry ingredients and mix well.

Drop 1 heaping tablespoon of dough at a time. Place on the prepared baking sheets, separated by a couple of inches. Do not overcrowd, as they spread while cooking. Sprinkle with the sesame seeds. Bake in the middle rack of the oven, until golden brown on top, 7 to 9 minutes. Make sure the bottoms do not burn.

Remove from the oven, transfer to a wire rack, and allow to cool completely. Serve immediately or store in an airtight container for 2 to 3 days.

Before homemade coconut ice cream became a staple in our house, I never imagined that it would taste even more satisfying than store-bought. It is much healthier too, as homemade ice cream has no gums, chemicals, or other additives. This recipe creates a creamy (but not too creamy) ice cream, closer to a gelato or sorbet, which allows the mixture of basil and strawberry flavors to really shine through.

STRAWBERRY BASIL ICE CREAM WITH PECAN CRUNCH

• • •

2 pounds strawberries, hulled and coarsely chopped

3 cups coconut milk

1 tablespoon vanilla extract

½ cup coconut palm sugar

1 cup fresh basil leaves

PECAN CRUNCH

½ cup pecans, coarsely chopped

1 tablespoon maple syrup

½ teaspoon vanilla extract

Pinch of fleur de sel (see Cook's Note, page 103)

SERVES 6 TO 8

Preheat the oven to 375°F. Put the strawberries in a single layer in a baking dish and bake in the oven until they have started to release their juices, 15 to 20 minutes. Remove from the oven and allow to cool completely.

Combine two-thirds of the strawberries and their juice, with the coconut milk, vanilla, coconut sugar, and basil in a high speed blender (refrigerate the rest of the strawberries to use for garnish). Blend on high until smooth, about 1 minute. Transfer to an ice cream maker and freeze according to the manufacturer's instructions. Transfer the ice cream to a glass container and freeze until firm, at least 2 hours. Before serving, leave the ice cream at room temperature for 30 minutes until soft enough to scoop.

While the ice cream is coming to room temperature, prepare the pecan crunch. Preheat the oven to 400°F. In a small roasting pan, mix the pecans with the maple syrup, vanilla, and fleur de sel. Roast in the oven until fragrant and well browned but not at all burnt, about 5 minutes. Allow to cool completely before using.

Serve the ice cream topped with the reserved strawberries and the toasted pecans.

Panna cotta is an Italian dessert made with dairy cream, milk, and white sugar, which is why it is usually bright white. This coconut panna cotta, on the other hand, is light brown; it's also easier to digest and much, much healthier. I don't mind the rich caramel color, and feel good knowing that all of the ingredients in this version are clean.

Feel free to use any kind of fresh fruit as a topping, there are no rules here.

KIWI COCONUT PANNA COTTA WITH CARAMELIZED PECANS

• • •

PANNA COTTA

3 cups coconut milk

1/3 cup coconut palm sugar

1 tablespoon plus
1 teaspoon agar agar flakes
(see Cook's Note)

Seeds from 2 vanilla beans,
or 1 tablespoon vanilla
extract

CARMELIZED PECANS

1/2 cup pecans, coarsely
chopped

1 tablespoon coconut
nectar

1/2 teaspoon vanilla extract

Pinch fleur de sel (see
Cook's Note, page 103)

5 kiwis, peeled and cubed

SERVES 4

To make the panna cotta, combine the coconut milk, coconut sugar, agar agar, and vanilla in a medium saucepan. Bring to a boil over medium heat, whisking vigorously and continuously to make sure the agar agar dissolves. Lower the heat and simmer, uncovered, for another 10 minutes, whisking frequently. Remove from the heat and set aside to cool. Divide the panna cotta among four cocktail or martini glasses and refrigerate until set, about 2 hours.

When the panna cotta is almost set, prepare the pecan garnish. Preheat the oven to 400°F. In a small roasting pan, combine the nuts with the coconut nectar, vanilla, and fleur de sel. Toast in the oven until fragrant and well browned, about 5 minutes. Transfer to a cutting board and allow to cool completely.

When the panna cotta has finished setting, sprinkle the kiwi and some of the pecans on top and serve.

🥄 **COOK'S NOTE** Agar agar is a mineral-rich sea vegetable used as a vegan substitute for gelatin. Agar agar flakes and powder can be found in most health food stores or grocery stores.

Although truffles are traditionally made out of chocolate, the word has come to accommodate any combination of ingredients that hold that characteristic round shape and size. In this recipe, almonds, dates, coconut oil, coconut sugar, and shredded coconut are combined to make a perfectly moist and flavorful treat without any refined sugars or processed ingredients. This is as healthy as a dessert can get!

Soaking the almonds overnight helps to remove the phytic acid and anti-nutrients contained within them. Phytic acid binds to minerals in the body and prevents their absorption. Wet almonds will not work in this recipe, so if you choose to soak, you will need to dehydrate them afterwards. You can do this in a dehydrator or your oven, on the lowest setting, for a couple hours (but the almonds will then no longer be raw). Rolling the truffles will leave your hands oily: just rub the oil into your skin—coconut oil makes a great moisturizer!

• • •

1 cup raw almonds, soaked overnight then dehydrated

4 dates, pitted

3 tablespoons coconut oil

2 teaspoons coconut sugar

2 teaspoons vanilla extract

¼ teaspoon sea salt

2 tablespoons shredded coconut

MAKES ABOUT 15

DATE AND ALMOND TRUFFLES

Place the almonds, dates, coconut oil, coconut sugar, vanilla, and sea salt in the bowl of a food processor. Process about 2 minutes, until you can pinch the mixture between your fingers and it holds together. If the mixture is still very loose after 2 minutes, add 1 or 2 more pitted dates and process again. You can also add 1 teaspoon of water to help the mixture stick together.

Using about 1 tablespoon of mixture at a time, roll the truffle mixture into small balls between your hands. Put the shredded coconut in a small bowl and roll the truffles in the shredded coconut until well coated.

Serve immediately or store in an airtight container for later use. The truffles will keep, refrigerated, for 2 weeks.

If sushi can be made out of white rice, brown rice, and even quinoa, why not black rice? Black rice is also known as forbidden rice, since in ancient China only emperors were allowed to eat it, and its cultivation was rare. Its dark grains cook to a deep purple shade that looks lovely on the plate. Highly nutritious, black rice is also easy to work with, and has a sticky quality that makes it ideal for sushi. Unlike other grains sometimes used in sushi, such as quinoa, black rice grains naturally stick together, but without turning to paste the way overly cooked white rice easily can.

BLACK RICE MANGO SUSHI

Combine the rice, coconut milk, coconut sugar, coconut vinegar, and salt in a medium saucepan and bring to a boil. Reduce the heat and simmer, covered, until the rice is sticky and no longer wet, about 15 minutes. Set aside to cool completely.

While the rice is cooking, make the sauce. Whisk together the coconut milk and coconut nectar. Set aside.

When the rice mixture is cool, lay a sheet of nori, shiny-side down on a sushi rolling mat (see Cook's Note). Place about 1/2 cup of the rice across the half of the sheet nearest you, leaving about 1/2 inch of nori exposed at the ends. Using wet fingers, press down to make sure the rice layer is of even thickness and stuck to the nori sheet. Place a generous amount of mango strips in the middle of the rice. Lift the end of the mat nearest you and start rolling the nori sheet over the ingredients, pressing down gently with the mat to make sure the roll is tight. When the roll is almost complete, dampen the rice on the top edge with wet fingers to seal the roll, and finish rolling. Lay the rolled sushi on a cutting board.

• • •

1 cup black rice, soaked overnight, drained and rinsed

1¼ cups coconut milk

¼ cup coconut palm sugar

2 tablespoons coconut vinegar or rice vinegar

½ teaspoon sea salt

⅓ cup coconut milk

1 tablespoon coconut nectar

6 sheets nori

1 large mango, sliced into thin strips

2 tablespoons shredded coconut, for garnish

SERVES 4 TO 6

Using a wet and very sharp knife, cut the roll into bite-sized pieces. If the knife starts to become sticky, wash it off before resuming cutting. Repeat with the rest of the nori sheets.

Arrange the sushi roll pieces on a platter. Sprinkle the tops with a little shredded coconut and serve immediately with the dipping sauce on the side.

COOK'S NOTE Sushi mats can be purchased in Japanese kitchen supply stores or online. Sushi rolls can also be made without a mat, by hand on a cutting board; it is just a little more difficult.

• • •

2 cups coconut milk

2 cups almond milk

½ cup chia seeds

4 tablespoons coconut
sugar

Seeds from 1 vanilla bean,
or 2 teaspoons vanilla
extract

1 teaspoon ground
cinnamon

Pinch of sea salt

3 cups blueberries

Seeds from 1 vanilla bean,
or 2 teaspoons vanilla
extract

½ cup toasted and
coarsely chopped almonds
(see Cook's Note, page 16)

1 tablespoon shredded
coconut

SERVES 4

Chia seeds are one of nature's superfoods. They functioned as high energy nourishment for the Aztecs, and are currently known as "the running food" because they are so good at helping long-distance runners maintain endurance. They help regulate blood sugar levels, are muscle and tissue builders, and are a superior source of protein. This pudding makes a very healthy and nutritious breakfast that can be prepared the night before and assembled in the morning. For a warm pudding, gently reheat on the stove before serving.

ALMOND VANILLA CHIA PUDDING WITH ROASTED BLUEBERRIES

To make the pudding, combine the coconut milk, almond milk, chia seeds, coconut sugar, vanilla, cinnamon, and salt in a large mason jar. Shake well. Put in the refrigerator and allow to thicken, at least 3 hours, and preferably overnight, whisking occasionally.

Preheat the oven to 350°F. Place the blueberries and vanilla in a small baking dish and mix well. Roast until soft and darker in color, 12 to 15 minutes. Remove from the oven and allow to cool for a couple of minutes before using

Serve the pudding topped with the toasted almonds, blueberries, and shredded coconut.

RESOURCES

WEBSITES
The Coconut Research Center, www.coconutresearchcenter.org, is a non-profit organization dedicated to educating the public about the benefits of coconut. It is operated by Bruce Fife, ND.

RECOMMENDED BRANDS AND SOURCES
Many of these ingredients can be found at Asian grocers, health food stores, or online.

Coconut Aminos Coconut aminos are a soy-free seasoning sauce made from coconut sap that has been aged and mixed with sea salt. I use the Coconut Secret brand (www.coconutsecret.com).

Coconut Butter Coconut butter (also sometimes called coconut manna) is basically concentrated coconut meat. I like the Artisana brand (www.artisanaorganics.com).

Coconut Cream I have had good results with the Native Forest brand.

Coconut Flour Coconut flour is finely ground dried, defatted coconut meat, which means that it is not only gluten-free, but also grain-free. My current favorite brand is Let's Do Organic.

Coconut Meat Coconut meat can be purchased packaged (usually in the frozen section of well-stocked grocery stores or in Asian markets). I like the Exotic Superfoods brand (www.exoticsuperfoods.com).

Coconut Milk My favorite brand is Aroy-D. When Aroy-D is not available, canned milk from Native Forest can also be used, as it is organic and comes in BPA-free cans.

Coconut Nectar Coconut nectar is the raw liquid sap of the coconut blossom. I like the Coconut Secret brand (www.coconutsecret.com).

Coconut Oil Always use organic, unrefined, raw (cold-pressed), virgin coconut oil, and store it at room temperature. My favorite brand is Artisana (www.artisanaorganics.com).

Coconut Palm Sugar There are many brands of good coconut palm sugar. Some of my favorites are Big Tree Farms (www.bigtreefarms.com), Navitas Naturals (www.navitasnaturals.com), and Wholesome Sweeteners (www.wholesomesweeteners.com).

Coconut Vinegar Coconut vinegar is naturally fermented coconut tree sap. Use raw, unfiltered and unpasteurized vinegar. I like the Coconut Secret brand (www.coconutsecret.com).

Coconut Water Whenever possible, use water taken straight from a fresh coconut, or buy raw, unpasteurized 100% coconut water with no additives. My favorite brand is Harmless Harvest (www.harmlessharvest.com), as its taste is closest to the real thing and it is raw, organic, and without additives.

BOOKS

Amsterdam, Elana. *Gluten-Free Cupcakes: 50 irresistible Recipes Made with Almond and Coconut Flour*. Berkeley, CA: Celestial Arts, 2011.

Enig, Mary and Sally Fallon. *Eat Fat, Lose Fat: The Healthy Alternative to Trans Fats*. New York: Plume, 2005.

Fallon, Sally. *Nourishing Traditions: The Cookbook that Challenges Politically Correct Nutrition and the Diet Dictocrats*. Washington, DC: New Trends Publishing, 2001.

Fife, Bruce. *Cooking with Coconut Flour: A Delicious Low-Carb, Gluten-Free Alternative to Wheat*. Colorado Springs, CO: Piccadilly Books, 2011.

Fife, Bruce. *The Coconut Oil Miracle*. New York: Avery Books, 2013.

McLagan, Jennifer. *Fat: An Appreciation of a Misunderstood Ingredient, with Recipes*. Berkeley, CA: Ten Speed Press, 2008.

Plank, Nina. *Real Food: What to Eat and Why*. New York: Bloomsbury, 2006.

Ravnskov, Uffe, MD, PhD. *Fat and Cholesterol are Good for You!* Sweden: GB Publishing, 2009.

Ross, Julia, MA *The Mood Cure: The 4-Step Program to Take Charge of Your Emotions—Today*. New York: Penguin, 2002.

Taubes, Gary. *Good Calories, Bad Calories: Fats, Carbs, and the Controversial Science of Diet and Health*. New York: Anchor Books, 2008.

ACKNOWLEDGMENTS

Thank you to my talented editor, Kelly Snowden, for her dedication to this book and for encouraging me to share my story. Thank you to Erin Scott, for her absolutely gorgeous photography; Lillian Kang, for her impeccable styling and respect for the ingredients; and Ashley Lima, for her talented art direction. You have all made the book come alive and I could not be more thrilled to have gotten to know you and worked with you.

To my husband, Ricardo, and our son, Luka, you have supported me and encouraged me beyond comprehension. I could not be more blessed and honored to be your wife, and your mother. Thank you.

To my friends and family who tasted, tested, and commented on countless recipes, thank you for your ruthless honesty and endless enthusiasm. I am thrilled to have you in my life and to finally show you the finished product.

ABOUT THE AUTHOR

Nathalie Fraise is a natural foods chef, nutrition educator, and the creator of the cooking app and food blog *Vanille Verte* (www.vanilleverte.com), where she shares tasty and healthy, nutrient-dense recipes. Her mission is to inspire people to reclaim their kitchen and cook for themselves and their families, as she firmly believes that this is the very best road to health and vibrancy.

INDEX

Ten Speed Press and the Ten Speed Press colophon are
registered trademarks of Penguin Random House LLC.

Library of Congress Cataloging-in-Publication Data is on file with the publisher.

Hardcover ISBN: 978-1-60774-805-2
eBook ISBN: 978-1-60774-806-9

Printed in China

Design by Ashley Lima
Food styling by Lillian Kang

10 9 8 7 6 5 4 3 2 1
First Edition